P

Sketchbook of Kansas Landmarks

Sketchbook of Kansas Landmarks

by

MARGARET WHITTEMORE

Illustrated by the Author

Published by
THE COLLEGE PRESS
Topeka, Kansas

COPYRIGHT 1936
BY MARGARET WHITTEMORE

CONTENTS

Foreword 9

Prehistoric Landmarks 11

Coronado in Kansas 15

On the Trail of the Indian 19

Forts of Frontier Days 25

Pioneer Trails 31

Hotels and Taverns 43

Sod Houses 49

Early Missions 53

Capitols of Kansas 59

Early Churches 67

Early Colleges 75

Early Libraries 83

John Brown of Kansas 87

Prohibition in Kansas 91

Steam and Water Mills 95

Primitive Windmills 103

Early Bridges 109

Historic Trees 117

First Oil Well in Kansas 125

STONE WINDMILL
Wamego, Kansas
From a Wood Block by Margaret Whittemore

FOREWORD

THE KANSAS STATE HISTORICAL SOCIETY has undertaken to mark the most noteworthy historic spots in Kansas. It has the co-operation of the Kansas Chamber of Commerce, the Sons and Daughters of the American Revolution, the Woman's Kansas Day Club and other organizations. As someone has said, "Such memorials serve the double purpose of awakening attention and of investing with an air of reality the events they perpetuate."

In this small volume it has been possible to include only a few of the points of historic interest, but it has been the aim to choose such as would help to give a cross-section of the background of our state. Early missions, capitols, events connected with the struggles of slavery days, the commerce of the trails, and other colorful features of Kansas' history have been emphasized.

The search for these relics of former days has been adventurous and enjoyable. A sketch-book serves as a license to trespass, to clamber over rough stones, climb over fences and peep in at cobwebbed windows. These sketches show, for the most part, the old buildings, trees, and bridges as they appear today, having weathered the storms of years.

Kansas may be justly proud of her record and of her people, and it is hoped that this volume may serve in a small way as a tribute to the hardy pioneers who laid the foundation of our state.

In 1929 *The Kansas Teacher* published a series of articles on historic landmarks of Kansas, and permission has been accorded to incorporate some of that material in this book. For their generous assistance in this undertaking thanks are due to the Kansas Chamber of Commerce, to Kirke Mechem, secretary of the Kansas State Historical Society, Kenneth K. Landis, assistant state geologist, and to other individuals who have offered helpful data. The author is appreciative of the courtesy of The Caxton Printers, Ltd., in granting permission to quote from "Sunbonnet Days" by Bliss Isely.

M. W.

THE SPHINX
Gove County

MONUMENT ROCKS
Gove County

10

MILLIONS OF YEARS AGO in what geologists call the Cretaceous time a branch of the sea extended up from the Gulf of Mexico north over what are now the Rocky Mountains. The eastern shore line stretched across eastern Kansas, and the western part of the state was under water. Great lizards and crocodiles slipped along the shores. The plesiosaur, a swimming reptile, had a length of forty or fifty feet, half of which was neck. There were eleven-foot turtles and birds with teeth. The world's largest insect, a primitive dragonfly, was discovered in 1935 as a fossil in Dickinson County. It is believed to have buzzed up and down the water one hundred and fifty million years ago.

When the sea waters ran off, the uptilting Kansas plains were exposed to the sun, wind and rain and many reactions set in. As a result we find today in certain sections strange formations of cretaceous chalk standing apart from each other as though carved by human hands, instead of the result of erosion. Where a chalk bed has been unusually hard, it has resisted erosion and served as a protective cap for the underlying rock.

About twenty-five miles south of Oakley in Gove County are interesting remnants of this uneven erosion, known as Monument Rocks or Pyramids. The loftiest rises to a height of some fifty feet. Ambitious climbers have reported finding on the flat tops immense shells, petrified seaweed and the fossils of large sea creatures. For many years an eagle had its nest on one of these rocks, and hawks frequently emerge from the crevices and circle around overhead. The formations are composed chiefly of magnesium and limestone. The chalk beds of western Kansas are now famous the world over for the fossils that have been discovered in them.

An early settler homesteaded the land upon which the pyramids stand, using the wall of one as a side to his little cabin. He failed to prove upon it, however, and the land reverted to the government. West of these rocks a few years ago one could see the ruins of old Fort Monument which in frontier days was used as a fortress against the approach of Indians. All around here bullets, cannon balls, buttons from army clothes, and other relics of early days have been picked up.

Among the Monument Rocks is one which presents the profile of a human face and is known as the "Sphinx." There she sits day in and day out. The place is relatively inaccessible and far from the highway that speeds the Colorado-bound vacationist across this area. The

11

CASTLE ROCK
Gove County

ROCK CITY
Ottawa County

12

Kansas sphinx was very old long before the Egyptian marvel was carved by man.

Rocks similar in formation to the pyramids may be seen in the Scott County State Park, and two miles from Arkansas City. Within easy driving distance of Hays is a spire known as "Castle Rock," rising about seventy-five feet in front of a series of canyons where beds of fossil specimens have been found. This is the tallest of the Smoky Hill buttes.

In Ellsworth County on the Union Pacific line is a large rock twenty-five or thirty feet high shaped like a gigantic mushroom. George Frances Train made a speech from the summit upon the completion of the railroad to this place.

A remarkable group of rock formations composes what is known as Rock City in Ottawa County. The stratification of these immense boulders is sharply marked. Many of them are large enough to fill a good-sized house. Weathering is slowly loosening portions of these reminders of the prehistoric past. The strange formations cover a field several acres in extent and offer unusual opportunities for the geologist in his study of the earth's surface and the changes which time brings.

In the western part of Barber and the eastern part of Comanche Counties the solvent effects of water on the gypsum are shown in several natural bridges and underground water courses whose roofs have partly fallen in. One of the most perfect of these is on Bear Creek, six miles south of Sun City. It spans the canyon of the creek and is about fifty-five feet from wall to wall. The height of the bridge above the bed of the creek is about twelve feet. The width at the middle is thirty-five feet. The upper surface declines to one side, but a wagon can be driven across it. Floods have torn at the natural arch and loosened great chunks of stone and soil until only a comparatively thin layer of rock joins the arch together at the top. As the stream is generally nearly dry one encounters no difficulty in walking underneath the bridge.

At this place there is also a cave, 260 feet long, cut through the bed of gypsum on the west bank of the stream. It is wide enough for a person to walk through. There are other caves nearby, all of which have been formed by underground water circulating through the rocks and dissolving out the soluble material.

QUIVIRA CABIN
Near Junction City

CORONADO HEIGHTS
Near Lindsborg

14

Coronado in Kansas

THE YEAR 1941 marks the four hundredth anniversary of the exploration of Kansas by Francisco Vasquez de Coronado, the first white man to set foot on the prairies of the Southwest. This was almost a century before the Pilgrims landed at Plymouth Rock. Coronado's visit is without doubt one of the most romantic bits of Kansas history.

During the past decade a wealth of material has been accumulated at Lyons, chiefly through the efforts of Paul A. Jones, who maintains that in Rice County were the cities of Cibola that Coronado was seeking. The remains of more than twenty Indian villages have been discovered along the streams of Rice County and are identified by the artifacts found upon them as the early homes of the Quivira Indians. These were the first agriculturally-minded settlers of the region. The many Quiviran relics that have been acquired by interested citizens of Lyons would in the aggregate make one of the most complete collections of the kind in existence. There are arrowheads, stones fashioned for tomahawks, jars, and several primitive corn-grinding implements.

A picturesque elevation near Lindsborg, known as "Coronado Heights," is one of a range of hills supposed to have been a lookout for the Spanish explorers in their march across Kansas. It is said that a piece of Coronado's armor was found there years ago. At any rate it is fitting that some piece of land in Kansas should be named for the Spanish conqueror. Daniel W. Wilder, in his "Annals of Kansas" deplored the fact that "as yet no county in our state bears the crowning name of its discoverer."

In 1881 Dr. John A. Udden of Bethany College at Lindsborg discovered through excavations a piece of Spanish chain mail and evidences of a prehistoric Indian village. Several years later the bronze point of a Spanish halberd or spear, sixteen and one-half inches long, was plowed up in a field in Barber County. It was decorated with leaves which came to spike-like points, a motif frequently used by Spanish architects of the sixteenth century. For that reason it is believed by some to have been left by a member of the Coronado expedition. Others believe it belonged to one of De Soto's men, since Coronado experienced none of the difficulty with the Indians that De Soto did. In 1935 it was placed in the museum of the Smithsonian Institution.

The first authentic account of the buffalo is given in Coronado's log, where he describes the plains as "full of crooked-back oxen," and adds, "They were a great succor for the hunger and want of bread which our people stood in."

One member of Coronado's party who served as chief historian of the trip has left a description of the land of the Quiviras, of the great river (the Arkansas) that was crossed, and has told of the grass dwellings. The Quiviras were the only Indians of the entire plains region who lived in grass huts. Consequently excavation reveals no walls, except foundation stones, and only rocks marking pathways.

About a century after Coronado visited this region the Sioux came down from the north and massacred most of the Quiviras and destroyed their villages. The last stand of these Indians is believed to have been at Wichita. Members of the Wichita tribe in Oklahoma are the lineal descendants of the Quiviras.

A Spanish priest, Juan de Padilla, in brown cassock and grass sandals, accompanied Coronado on his expedition. Although a horse was offered him, the young Franciscan preferred to plod along on foot. When, after two years' rambling, Coronado returned to Mexico, Father Padilla, fired by missionary zeal, remained on the plains to preach the gospel to the Indians. He is said to have converted twenty-five thousand Quiviras to Christianity. They held him in high reverence.

One morning in 1542, as he knelt in prayer, some savage Indians attacked the priest and he was slain, becoming the first Christian martyr in this western country. Friendly Indians buried him, marking the spot with a great heap of stones. Margaret Hill McCarter has paid tribute to this missionary in her book, *In Old Quivira*. In 1904 a monument was erected in Herington by the Quivira Historical Society on the spot where it is supposed Padilla was slain. The Council Grove Historical Society has placed a permanent marker at his early grave.

Three other monuments commemorating events connected with the Coronado expedition have been placed by the Quivira Historical Society. They are in Geary, Riley and Wabaunsee Counties. In a park in Manhattan a monument has been erected to Tatarrax, chief of the Harahey Indians, who visited with Coronado when he led his party into Kansas. The Harahey tribe is honored by another monument at Alma.

A granite obelisk, erected in 1902 by Captain Robert Henderson in Logan Grove, two miles south of Junction City, marks the place which J. V. Brower, Minnesota archæologist, concluded was the end of Coronado's quest. Mr. Brower had himself tramped over Coronado's trail and believed this to be the site of a great Quivira village. The

16

grove has yielded flints, a kiln, the skeleton of a chieftain, and other indications of Indian occupancy.

Logan Grove was homesteaded in 1857 by Captain Henderson, who at the age of seventeen had left his home in Belfast, Ireland, to make the six-weeks voyage to America on a sailing vessel. He joined the army and was sent to Texas to fight Indians. On the Texas frontier, when his command was isolated in an Indian camp with no hope of reenforcement, he volunteered to ride three hundred miles through the Indian country for additional troops. His horse was shot from under him but he stole another and got through. His knowledge of astronomy enabled him to travel at night.

As a reward for his valor, Henderson received a land warrant for "160 acres anywhere in the United States." His company was ordered to Fort Riley in 1855 and when he saw this beautiful grove he knew it was the land of his choice. He preempted adjoining territory until his acres totaled one thousand.

The log cabin had been built many years before this by some white man, probably a hunter or trapper. In 1853 it was discovered by a Mr. Chivers, who sold it two years later to Henderson for ten dollars.

After his discharge in 1857, Henderson took his bride to live in the cabin. Later he cut down some of his finest walnut trees and built the first big house in Junction City. There his family lived while he fought in the Civil War. He was many times cited for bravery. Meanwhile the little cabin was used at various times as a fort, a church, a schoolhouse, a political meeting-place, a mortuary and a residence. The grove in which it stands was named for General John A. Logan, a personal friend of Captain Henderson.

The Earl C. Gormley Post No. 45 of the American Legion has now bought Logan Grove and it is to become a public park. It is said to be the finest oak grove in Kansas today. The age of the largest trees has been estimated at one hundred and fifty years.

BURNETT'S MOUND
Near Topeka

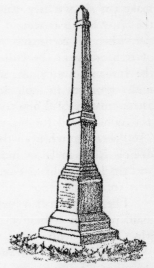

MONUMENT MARKING SITE OF
PAWNEE INDIAN VILLAGE
Republic County

INDIAN CAVES
Wabaunsee County

On the Trail of the Indian

AMONG KANSAS' STATE-OWNED possessions is a natural amphi-theater near Medicine Lodge in Barber County where the United States government and five tribes of plains Indians signed peace treaties in 1867, opening western Kansas to white settlement and permitting the building of railroads to the Pacific coast. The five tribes represented were Kiowas, Comanches, Apaches, Cheyennes and Arapahoes. There were about five thousand Indians present. Bull Bear, chief of the Cheyennes, stated the case for the Indians, explaining that they owned the country and did not want railways built through it to scare away the buffalo.

When the treaties were finally concluded they provided reservations for all the tribes in exchange for Kansas and Colorado. Except for one or two small raids at a later date, these treaties practically ended Indian warfare in Kansas.

Every five years a pageant is held in this amphitheater in commemor-ation of the event. In 1931 the Kansas legislature voted to set aside four hundred acres here as a state park and appropriated ten thousand dollars to buy and properly prepare the great amphitheater for enjoy-ment by the people.

The village of the Pawnees in Republic County was visited by Zebulon M. Pike in 1806. He was on an exploration trip with a small party of soldiers when he reached the Pawnee Indian village. He met with the grand council of the Pawnees on September 29 and ordered the chief to haul down the Spanish flag flying over the council chamber. It had been left there by a party of Spaniards.

When the chief ignored the request, Lieutenant Pike insisted that it was impossible for the Indians to have two fathers. The chief then took down the Spanish emblem and laid it at the officer's feet and hoisted the Stars and Stripes in its place. This was the first time the American flag ever waved in Kansas.

In 1901 the state erected on the site a shaft of Barre, Vermont, granite, twenty-six feet high. A movement is under way to convert the historic spot into a national park.

Kansas has several mounds and rocks noted because of their associa-tion with the redskins. Midway between Great Bend and Larned in Barton County, Pawnee Rock rises abruptly out of a fertile stretch of bottom land. The name of the rock was taken from a great fight lasting several days between the Pawnees and the plains Indians.

This huge pile of reddish volcanic stone covers about five acres. The northern and western slopes are covered with loose soil, while the south and east are bare and sheer in their ascent from the plain. The rock is a quarter mile north of the old Santa Fe Trail and was a favorite stopping point due to its being easily defended in case of trouble with the Indians. It afforded a peaceful shelter for the weary traveler where he might quench his thirst at the spring flowing from its base. The early settlers quarried much of the rock.

On July 13, 1846, Colonel Doniphan planted the American flag on the rock and left it there. Thousands of names have been inscribed upon the face of the rock and there are several Indian paintings. Included among the inscriptions are names of "forty-niners" and others whose lives are a part of the early history of the state. Many date back one hundred and fifty years.

The Woman's Kansas Day Club in 1908 started a movement to make this a state park. The development includes construction of a stone gateway and wall, an observation tower on top of the rock, a flagpole and a memorial monument. The latter has already been erected "in honor of the brave men and women who passing over the Santa Fe Trail endured the hardship of frontier life and blazed the path of civilization for posterity."

Burnett's Mound near Topeka was named in honor of Abraham Burnett, a Pottawatomie chief, who lived on a farm at the foot of the hill. He weighed four hundred and fifty pounds and possessed great physical strength. For many generations the Indians used this mound as a vantage point for observation and signalling. From 1849 to 1854 it served as a landmark, dividing the Oregon and the California-bound emigrants. Because the trails diverged here, Topeka was the final trading-post where wagon trains could lay in their supplies before the long last lap of their journey.

This mound is said to mark the final halting place of the great glaciers that swept down over America thousands of years ago. Geologists, in investigating the region, have found groups of glacial deposits called terminal moraines and hard rocks gathered by the glacier and carried along by it. The glacier seems to have stopped at the northern slope of the mound.

Geologists say that the glaciers advanced down over North America at least five times. The second, known as the Kansas glacier, came the farthest, for the others did not extend farther south than northern

Iowa. The Kansas glacier is estimated to have come four hundred and ten thousand years ago.

Four miles east of Peabody is Indian Guide Hill on which a monument has been erected to commemorate the use of the eminence as a guide post in the prairie country.

Ruins of the only Indian pueblo ever built in this state have been located in Scott County, ten miles south of the Smoky Hill River. El Quartelejo, as it was called, was established in 1604 by certain families of Picurie Indians from Taos, New Mexico, who were fleeing from Spanish oppression. They remained in this region, farming the valley along Beaver Creek, until the Spanish government sent Juan de Archeluta to bring them back to their former homes.

The pueblo was originally a fortified stone and adobe building, measuring thirty-two by fifty feet, and divided into seven rooms. It was probably the first walled house ever constructed within the present borders of Kansas. Prior to 1720, after the Indians left it to return to New Mexico, it was used as a French trading-post. It finally burned and the ruins were discovered by a farmer. The spot was appropriately marked in 1925 by the Kansas Society of the D. A. R.

Near this place a sword of Spanish make was found on which in almost obliterated letters is the name of one of Coronado's officers. It is preserved in the museum of the Kansas State Historical Society.

Burial grounds of these Indians are believed to have been found about half a mile from the site of El Quartelejo. Workmen engaged in building a road in March, 1935, uncovered two skeletons buried on a hillside in a sitting position. Several days later three more graves were unearthed with the bodies buried in the same manner. Although the Indians' irrigation ditches have easily been traced, this is the first sign ever found of their burial ground.

In the northeast corner of McPherson County in the Marquette cliffs is a natural corral where other Indian tribes are said to have hidden their horses. The place is secluded and not easy to find.

Great Spirit Spring in Mitchell County was discovered by Lieutenant Pike on his way west to Colorado and Idaho. Many tribes of Indians knew of the spring for centuries, long before the white man came upon the scene. To them it possessed a mysterious charm. They held their pow-wows around it, dipped their arrows into the pool, and, judging by many relics found in the water, undoubtedly tried to propitiate the Great Spirit by casting articles into its limpid waters.

EL QUARTELEJO PUEBLO MARKER
Scott County State Park

PAWNEE ROCK
Barton County

HURON CEMETERY
Kansas City

22

Many legends cluster about it, one to the effect that Waconda the daughter of a great chief, loved the son of the chief of a hostile tribe. The intimacy was frowned upon by the parents of both, but the lovers paid no attention to their elders. Finally the tribes met on the plain surrounding the spring and a battle ensued.

The lover of Waconda, weak from loss of blood, fell headlong into the depths of the pool. When the maiden, frantic with grief, turned upon her father and charged him with the murder of the young brave, he bent his bow, sending an arrow through her skull. Her body followed that of her lover into the spring. And thus the place received its name, Waconda.

Located on a mound, forty-two feet high, the spring is a puzzle to geologists. It is fed from saliferous shales overlying Dakota sandstone three hundred to eight hundred feet below the surface. The water does not flow away as does that in ordinary springs, due to the porous rock affording innumerable outlets for it to escape as fast as the subterranean inlets feed it. Originally the spring is said to have overflowed from the top by a gentle seepage toward the south. It is generally believed to be bottomless.

Trading Post, on the Marais des Cygnes river, was established by Giareau, a Frenchman, who began trading with the Indians as early as 1834. The site is marked with a bronze tablet.

When by a treaty in 1855 the Wyandottes were given the right of claiming citizenship in the United States they ceded their lands to the government to be platted and deeded individually to the tribesmen. One portion of land which they withheld for a burial ground was a tract of about two acres, now known as Huron Cemetery. There were probably four hundred burials here between 1844 and 1855.

This cemetery is now in the very center of the business district of Kansas City, Kansas, and has been the subject of many court battles. Congress finally appointed a commission to sell the plot, but objections by surviving Wyandottes were so strong and aroused so much public sentiment against the sale that a suit was brought to stop it. The case finally reached the Supreme Court, which upheld the bill of Congress. However public opinion still maintains place for this cemetery in the heart of the city and it has never been sold.

On the south wall of Bartell House in Junction City a bronze plaque bears this inscription: "This tablet marks the site of a stone building where early-day settlers of Junction City in 1861 took refuge from a raid of 9,000 Indians who were holding a war dance, with fresh scalps dangling from the bridles of their ponies."

At Oberlin in Decatur County, a monument has been erected to the memory of pioneers killed in the Indian massacre of 1878, and also as a marker of the last Indian raid in Kansas. On September 30, 1878, a band of four hundred northern Cheyennes led by Chief Dull Knife made the last raid into Kansas, killing nineteen settlers in Decatur County. These Indians had spent two weeks in crossing the state from south to north, committing many depredations. The monument marked the thirty-third anniversary of the end of the Indians' destruction in Kansas, and their final disappearance over the state line.

The town site of Emporia was bought from the Kaw Indians, and the town was founded in the spring of 1857. The white men who laid it out made an agreement among themselves that anyone allowing gambling or selling of liquor should forfeit his right to any land. The government allowed a half-section of land for the town. The area from Sixth Avenue north was known as Indian Territory.

In eastern Kansas, six miles southwest of Ottawa, are the Chippewa hills, romantic because of their Indian traditions. The earliest known inhabitants, who came about 1830, were Indians, and later came trappers and missionaries. The history of the Chippewas, since 1860, has been intimately connected with that of the Munsee tribe, which came in that year from near Leavenworth to live with them. The two tribes established a sort of communal life back in those hills. There are today only a few half-breed families living in the hills, which have become quite wild and desolate. An old mission church still stands, but it is occupied only by some very active and belligerent hornets that guard well its interior and the surrounding grounds.

On U. S. Highway 50S has been erected a monument honoring Major Robert H. Chilton because of his success in keeping order among the plains Indians during the period between the Mexican and Civil wars. Many an Indian depredation was forestalled by his diplomacy, strategy and generalship.

24

Forts of Frontier Days

*A*S CIVILIZATION MOVED westward, numerous forts were established in Kansas at frequent intervals to protect the inhabitants from Indian attacks.

In 1818 when the government determined to establish a military post at the mouth of the Yellowstone River, as one of a system of forts in the west, Cow Island was selected as a winter camp and base of provisions for this undertaking. Accordingly, Cantonment Martin was established here in 1819, the first military post in Kansas.

Cow Island, or Isle au Vache, was named by the French who discovered it in the eighteenth century. It is a fertile tract of about one thousand acres, midway between Atchison and Leavenworth. Although the flood of 1881 changed the channel of the river, placing the island on the Missouri side, it is still Kansas soil, as tried and determined in court. It was the scene of many Indian councils and the place where Lewis and Clark fired the first gun on Kansas soil in commemoration of the Fourth of July.

In early days there were five forts in Ford County within a few miles of each other, although Fort Dodge is the only one still existing, and that only as a State Soldiers' Home. The other forts in the county were Fort Mann, Fort Atkinson, Fort Mackey and Fort Arkansas.

Colonel Henry I. Dodge, of the United States Army, left Fort Leavenworth in 1835 on an expedition to the Rocky Mountains. Arriving at the north bank of the Arkansas River about five miles below where Dodge City now is located, he established a fort, known as "Dodge." The first adobe buildings were later replaced by others of stone, a few of which are still standing.

When the fort was abandoned in 1882, the government left the property in charge of a custodian who allowed the enclosure to be used as a cattle corral. The reservation originally consisted of thirty thousand acres purchased from the Osage Indians. Part of this land was surveyed and sold to settlers to be used as cattle and farming land.

Dodge City, the "Cowboy Capital," laid out in 1872, attracted buffalo hunters and frontiersmen, for the cattle drive in Kansas was then in full swing. During the herding season the cowboy rode seventy miles a day and was considered the finest horseman in the world. In his clanking spurs and huge sombrero he excelled in all the rude sports of the field, and although rough and uncouth, he was often brave and generous. He liked to appear rougher than he really was. The streets

COWBOY STATUE ON BOOT HILL
Dodge City

FORT LEAVENWORTH WALL
Near Leavenworth

26

were lined with rugged pioneers, romantic, picturesque characters, as well as with an overplus of swaggering pirates and gun-toting free-booters.

In the heart of what is now a modern city is Boot Hill, the burial ground for those adventurers who passed away with their boots on. In the brief funeral accorded them their boots were not removed. A Cowboy Statue made of cement by the late Dr. O. H. Simpson, a dentist of Dodge City, was erected on Boot Hill by the city commission some years ago. On the base of the statue is carved the allegorical epigram: "On the ashes of my camp-fire this city is built."

On the old Fort Dodge-Fort Hays trail in northeastern Hodgeman County at Duncan's Crossing on the Pawnee River, women of the community have erected a monument dedicated to the pioneers who traveled this historic route. It is located on the spot where the first post-office in that part of the country was opened by George Duncan.

Fort Larned was one of the important military posts during the years when Indians were preying on overland trains between Independence and Santa Fe. It was established in 1859 in Pawnee County and was first known as "The Camp on Pawnee Fork," being located on that tributary to the Arkansas River. The name was later changed to Camp Alert, because the soldiers stationed there had to be on constant guard against prowling Indians. It was finally called Fort Larned in honor of Colonel B. F. Larned, paymaster-general.

Troops from Fort Larned quelled the Wichita and Osage Indians during the excitement caused by railroads invading the choice hunting grounds in western Kansas. By 1878 the Indians had been removed to Indian Territory and it was thought best to abandon the fort. The arsenal, stables, quarters of the officers and mess-rooms still stand and are used for farm purposes. Although the buildings have been repaired, they are not materially altered.

Fort Riley was established in 1852 to protect the trade of the Santa Fe Trail. It was known as Camp Center until 1855, being near the center of the United States. In that same year Congress definitely established it as a cavalry post and directed the engineers to plan the construction of a training school for cavalry units of the army. For many years Fort Riley was the headquarters of General Custer and his famous Seventh Cavalry.

Major E. A. Ogden was the first officer in charge. The Ogden monument, erected in his memory by quarrymen, teamsters, stone-

GUARD HOUSE
Fort Scott

BLOCK HOUSE
Fort Hays

28

cutters and laborers, is one of the outstanding features of the reservation. Near the center of the post is the Wounded Knee monument. It was erected in memory of the troops killed at the Battle of Wounded Knee in South Dakota where cavalry from Fort Riley were sent to quell a Sioux Indian uprising. The monument was dedicated by comrades of the twenty-five soldiers slain.

Fort Leavenworth was established in 1827 by Colonel Henry Leavenworth for the protection of the Santa Fe traders from the invasions of Indians who were raiding and plundering the caravans. The first post-office in Kansas Territory was established here under the name "Cantonment Leavenworth" in 1828. This was the starting point for many famous expeditions in the '40s. It was designated as the temporary seat of government for Kansas Territory in 1854.

A bronze statue of General Ulysses S. Grant by Lorado Taft was unveiled at the fort in 1899. It was the first of the kind to be erected in the west to an officer of the United States Army.

Just north of this statue stands part of an old wall built in 1827 as a defense against the Indians. A marker was placed here by the Capt. Jesse Leavenworth chapter of the D. A. R. in 1917. There are some thirty-two narrow slits about twenty inches high through which the guards could shoot. These are about a yard apart. There is one wider opening. The wall is quite thick, with the openings on the north side much wider, enabling one to take better aim with his rifle, and yet be protected from attack.

Fort Hays, located southeast of the present city of Hays, was established in 1865 under the name of Fort Fletcher. Here the intrepid Custer once made his headquarters for warfare against the Indians. Early in 1867 William F. Cody, better known as "Buffalo Bill," established the town of Rome, a mile west of Hays. It is said that he had visions of great wealth as the tide of emigration moved westward; but he was doomed to disappointment for, although Rome flourished for a time, it was abandoned in favor of Hays which the railroad reached in October of that year.

In 1901 Congress deeded the site of the old fort to the state of Kansas for educational and park purposes. An experiment station and normal school were established on part of the land. The latter developed into the Fort Hays Kansas State College. In 1929 a state public park was created on the site. Two of the original stone buildings of the fort are still standing, the guardhouse and the blockhouse.

Fort Zarah was established in 1864 three miles east of Great Bend in the Walnut valley. A few years after its abandonment in 1869 all of the stone in the buildings was appropriated by early settlers in the neighborhood. Two depressions remained marking the site of the two buildings which were connected by an underground tunnel for use in case of an Indian attack. The banks of Walnut Creek still show traces of rifle pits thrown up for the purpose of defense from Indian assault. Near the old fort is a marker in the form of an obelisk surmounted by a Civil War cannon, erected as a monument by the pennies of school children of Barton County.

Fort Scott reveres its past and has held, untouched by modernism, the buildings that link it with the early years. Two or three blocks from the business section are buildings erected nearly one hundred years ago by General Winfield Scott as a military post for protection against unruly Indians. There is a plaza on which General Scott paraded his soldiers. On it stands the old log guardhouse with niches cut through its thick walls for the rifle barrels of the soldiers. There is a stable, said to be of native walnut, in which the cavalry horses were kept. Other frame buildings were used as offices, barracks and dining halls. These long ago passed into private hands, but the guardhouse is owned and maintained by the city. This fort was built on the military road the government maintained to link the western forts and over which it moved its supplies. It was abandoned in 1865.

Fort Harker was used for a long time as a shipping point of freight for New Mexico on the Santa Fe Trail. During the building of the Union Pacific Railroad, Fort Wallace in Wallace County was an important post. The railroad was completed to the fort in July, 1868, and during the following year several skirmishes occurred with the Indians. Other forts established in the state were Fort Lincoln on the Osage River; Fort Aubrey, one hundred miles from Fort Dodge; and Fort Camp Jewell on the site of Jewell City.

*T*HE OREGON TRAIL was the path of the home-seeker — the trail that built our empire to the west. It followed the course of least resistance, for it was originally the track of the wild animals on their seasonal migration for grasses. It was the teepee road of the Indian, the road of the fur-trader and trapper, and the route of the Pony Express riders. It was a path made by nature and utilized by man.

On April 10, 1830, Jedediah Strong Smith with his partners, Jackson and Sublette, and about eighty other fur-traders, trappers and attendants, left St. Louis in mule-drawn wagons bound for a rendez-vous in the Rocky Mountains. They demonstrated that it was possible to make the trip and return in six months or less.

This first wagon trip over a large part of the Oregon Trail was followed by the journey of Captain Bonneville with his ox-team train two years later; then that of Nat Wyeth, a Boston cod-fisherman; and the romantic journey of Dr. Marcus Whitman and Rev. H. H. Spalding with their brides, the first white women to cross the continent over the Oregon Trail.

The north branch of this trail ran through Doniphan, Brown, Nemaha and Marshall Counties and across the northwest corner of Washington County, then turned into Nebraska and followed the Platte River westward. The southern branch entered Kansas at West-port and ran south of the Kansas River through Johnson, Douglas and Shawnee Counties, crossing the river at Papan's Ferry in Topeka. It ran through Pottawatomie and Marshall Counties to the crossing of the Big Blue at Marysville, where it joined the branch from St. Joseph.

The town of Marysville dates back to 1846 when Francis J. Mar-shall settled on the Oregon Trail establishing a trading-post, store, post-office and ferry. This was the last place within the present limits of Kansas where letters could be mailed for points east. Marshall charged one dollar each for mailing them at St. Joseph. Ferry charges were three dollars for each wagon. In 1855, after Kansas was thrown open to settlement, Marshall started the town of Marysville, naming it for his wife. This was a station on the Pony Express line in 1860 and 1861 and also an eating station on Ben Holladay's Overland Stage line.

An Oregon Trail marker, purchased by citizens of Marshall county through the sale of memorial half dollars, has been dedicated in the city park of Marysville. It is a huge boulder in which a copper plate is inserted. The town of Bremen in the same county has also erected a marker on which is inscribed:

LEST WE FORGET
OREGON TRAIL
1827-1875

At a point a little west of the present town of Gardner a signboard was set up in early days to show where the Oregon and Santa Fe trails divided. It said, "Road to Oregon."

A simple but handsome granite stone gleams brightly in the sunshine on the dividing line between Kansas and Nebraska, two miles west of Lanham, Nebraska. It is on the old Oregon Trail and was dedicated with fitting ceremonies in 1914.

The trail is being marked along its entire route by chapters of the D. A. R. It was in 1852 that the late Ezra Meeker first followed the trail. He again crossed the country in his eighty-first year to rediscover and map it throughout its entire course. For more than one thousand miles he found that it had become almost obliterated. Only one stretch of four hundred miles was indelibly marked. By relying on his memory and with the aid of government surveyors, he was able to reconstruct the route throughout its entire length.

It lay over sterile prairies, barren deserts, and seemingly impassable mountain ranges, and required fording and refording numerous streams. Oxen journeyed at the rate of two miles an hour, averaging about twelve or fifteen miles a day. Four forts were established on the trail to guard it. Although the government did not contribute anything for the construction or preservation of the Oregon Trail, it nevertheless became a great highway. It was sometimes called the "California Road."

As a result of this early movement, the United States pushed its claims to Oregon, and in 1845 a treaty was signed with Great Britain giving this nation all the land north to the forty-ninth parallel. After 1844 the trail was crowded with settlers and home seekers. In 1849 gold was discovered in California and all other migrations were eclipsed by the "rush" at that time.

Two years previous the Mormons began their successive treks to the "Promised Land" beside the Great Salt Lake, where they founded their colony. Some of them followed the Oregon Trail, but there was also the Mormon Trail, commencing at Little Santa Fe, Missouri, and ending at Salt Lake. This trail passed about six miles southwest of

32

Topeka, going over Burnett's Mound, across the Shunganunga, on by Dr. Lykin's farm, across Mill Creek and directly through the Rev. Robert Simmerwell's fields.

In 1905 the Kansas legislature appropriated one thousand dollars for the purpose of procuring suitable monuments to mark the Santa Fe Trail. Under the supervision of the regent of the D. A. R. and the secretary of the State Historical Society this trail has been appropriately and adequately marked across the entire length of the state. Other roads were used in reaching western points besides the real trail followed by the government.

From Leavenworth trains left for Santa Fe by two different routes. One came by Indianola, crossing the Kaw at Topeka, sometimes by Papan's Ferry and at other times fording the river a little above where the Rock Island Railroad bridge now stands. Thence it ran southwest by Auburn, crossing the Wakarusa at three different points, and joining the Independence trail at Wilmington. The other route from Leavenworth came across the Delaware Reserve by Tonganoxie, crossing the Kaw at Lawrence, and striking the Independence branch near Overbrook.

After Wilmington there were no deviations in the route until it reached the Arkansas River. Here one trail followed up the river, going past the point where Fort Dodge now stands. The other followed a cut-off over the hills striking the river at what was called "the lower Cimarron crossing," going over the Horn Alley to the Cimarron River, on by Cold Springs, Rabbit Ear, the Canadian or Red River, by the Wagon Mound, and on to Fort Union. Another trail followed up to the Aubrey or middle crossing of the river, going over to Bear Creek, thirty-five miles, and striking the Cimarron trail near Cold Springs.

Marks left by the trail can still be traced in many places as clearly as if made yesterday. This is especially true in the vicinity of Auburn. Near Elkhart the deep ruts made in the soil along the bluffs north and east of the "Point of Rocks" monuments by the wheels of the great wagons loaded with goods for Santa Fe trade remain imbedded in the yellow ground at depths varying from two to six feet. At a point eight miles west of Elkhart, just across the line in eastern Colorado, the deep depressions made by the passage of great droves of longhorn cattle following the annual round-ups in Texas when driven north to Wyoming and Montana, are yet visible in the soil after a period of almost fifty years.

LAST CHANCE STORE
Council Grove

PONY EXPRESS STATION
Marysville

34

For nearly a century after Coronado's expedition no white man appears to have crossed the plains. In 1804 a Frenchman named La Lande was sent as an agent by an Illinois merchant on a trading trip to Santa Fe. He made the trip safely and was followed in 1805 by James Pursley, an American trader. Both of these men remained in New Mexico.

In 1806 Lieutenant Zebulon Pike was sent into the territory to deal with the Indians and make maps of the country. The published account of this expedition gave the initial impulse to the trade movement over the Santa Fe Trail, and before long a definite line of communication was established between Santa Fe and the Missouri border towns.

From 1812 to 1824 most of the commerce over the old trail was by pack-mule trains. After that the ox-wagon period set in and continued until 1848 when the stagecoach became general. The prairie schooner was so called because the bodies of these vehicles actually resembled boats.

The huge wagons used for the transportation of goods and government supplies were loaded with six or seven thousand pounds at Independence or at Leavenworth. Six yoke of cattle were hitched to each wagon. Trains were started as early as possible in the spring, depending on the grass situation, as the oxen had to live on grass altogether. A train consisted of twenty-six wagons. A full crew was twenty-nine men — twenty-six drivers, boss, assistant boss and an extra. The two bosses were mounted on mules.

Frank M. Stahl of Burlingame, who twice followed the trail to Santa Fe, gives the following account:

"Many times the start was made for the morning drive by the time it began to show light. There was an early drive of three or four miles before breakfast. The oxen grazed until after noon when they were driven in and yoked up and driven four or five miles further, unyoked and turned out to graze again. About four o'clock we had supper — only two meals each day. The oxen were yoked up and another four or five miles made. Then they were unyoked and turned out for the night. Two men were detailed as night herders.

"There were no streams bridged and often, on account of wagons being stuck in the mud, progress was slow. Sometimes the entire day was consumed in crossing a stream. It generally took a day to cross the Neosho at Council Grove. This was the last place where supplies could be obtained before reaching Fort Union in New Mexico.

"Wood for cooking purposes could be obtained until we struck Ash Creek, just below where Fort Larned was later located. This was the last place for wood for hundreds of miles, so of course it was husbanded very carefully. Each wagon had a large gunny sack nailed to the side to be filled by the drivers with buffalo chips during the day.

"The crossing of the Arkansas River was always a 'red letter day,' especially at the Cimarron crossing. At this point the river was nearly a mile in width, and in one place for some eighty feet, three and a half feet deep. For the crossing thirty-two cattle were hitched to each wagon. One man was detailed to steer the lead cattle in each team through the deep water. Several yoke of cattle were in the deep water all the time while crossing, and unable to pull to amount to anything. It generally took an entire day to cross. After crossing there were about four miles of heavy sand before solid ground was reached. In this stretch the teams had to double. After reaching solid ground the cattle were driven back to the river and watered."

It is said that when leaving the outfitting stations at Independence and Westport it was customary for each party to take with it an extra wagon, dividing its parts up among the wagons as needed — a wheel here, the tongue there, and the bed taken apart and distributed likewise. On one expedition this extra wagonbed was sunk in the spring at the Cimarron crossing in order to give a supply of clear water. When the party moved on, it was decided to leave the wagonbed in the spring. The result was that the companies following the trail came to refer to the springs as "Wagonbed Springs," and the name lasted long after the wood of the wagonbed had been worn away.

Felix Xavier Aubrey, a French Canadian, is ranked as the supreme rider in the great riding tradition of the west. The story of his eight-hundred-mile ride over the old Santa Fe Trail has become history. It generally took horsemen from three to four weeks to go from Santa Fe to Independence, but Aubrey announced in 1848 that he would make the trip in eight days. Bets ran high. Although it took him eight days and ten hours to make the trip, his actual traveling time was about seven days if one counts out the time he was detained by Indians.

When Aubrey returned to Santa Fe in the late summer, he heard Kit Carson and others discussing his record ride.

"I can do better," he said. "I bet one thousand dollars that I can make the ride within six days."

He at once began to make preparations. He sent three or four men ahead with relay horses so that at Fort Mann on the Arkansas and at

Council Grove he could rely on getting fresh mounts. On the morning of September 12, he left Santa Fe in a swinging gallop and stopped neither to eat nor to sleep. He ate while riding and after the first day and night tied himself to the saddle so that he could doze without danger of falling off. Although it was the rainy season of the year and six hundred miles of the trail were muddy and every stream across the distance was swollen, he won his wager and had several hours to spare. On this trip he used eleven horses. There were two skirmishes with Indians and an arrow went through his arm. His route was thereafter called the Aubrey Trail.

Abilene was known throughout the country in the latter '60s as a shipping point for Texas cattle. In 1867 the first herd of long-horned steers was driven up from Texas to be sold here. Credit for the establishment of Abilene as a terminus for the cattle trail is given Joseph G. McCoy, who came there in 1867. He placed signs that marked the cattle trail in part of Kansas. In July of the same year a civil engineer marked a trail through Dickinson, Marion, Sedgwick, and Sumner Counties to the Indian Territory, varying it from right to left to secure good watering and camping places to accommodate large herds of cattle and the necessary men attending them. The marking consisted of small mounds of turf. In 1925 a boulder waas placed at Abilene with this inscription: "This boulder marks the northern terminus of the Texas Cattle Trail over which in 1867-1871 journeyed herds numbering more than 3,000,000 head, and it was dedicated to the Pioneers of Abilene in recognition of their achievements. Placed by the Abilene Chapter of the D. A. R."

When the Wichita Indians lived on the Arkansas River at the mouth of the Little Arkansas, Jesse Chisholm, a noted mixed-blood Cherokee, located there to trade with them. In the early spring of 1865 he invited another trader to join him in a venture, following a trail that had been laid out several years before by Black Beaver of the Delaware tribe. It was known eventually as "the Chisholm Trail," and since it coincided for a distance of two hundred miles with the Texas Cattle Trail, the name of Chisholm came to be applied also to the cattle trail. The Chisholm Trail was, however, more than merely a cattle trail. It was a highway of travel and communication. A telegraph line was strung along it from the end of the railroad at Caldwell years before the railroad was built southward from the Kansas line. Stage stations and camping places were scattered along the line of the trail. On the heels of the immigrant came the Rock Island surveyors, setting the

SANTA FE TRAIL MARKER
Olathe

ERECTED BY JOHNSON
and the
OLD SETTLER'S ASSOCIATION
1907

KANSAS OR BUST

PRAIRIE SCHOONER

stakes for a railway line. It was built near the old trail, sometimes even obliterating its traces and appropriating its once busy and dusty site.

Among the historic state lines and trails of Kansas is the old Leavenworth military road or the Butterfield Overland stage route, which was the shortest and at one time practically the only road between Denver and Leavenworth. Before it was mapped out as a stage line and military road it was an Indian trail. On March 3, 1853, Congress authorized that the trail be made a military road between Leavenworth and Fort Riley. It passed through Salt Creek, Easton, Indianola, Silver Lake, Manhattan and Junction City. The Butterfield Overland dispatch route was laid out over the trail in 1859 and extended to Denver and La Porte where it struck the Overland stage route.

Overland stages began running from Atchison to Placerville, California, in 1860. The fare was twelve cents a mile, each passenger being allowed twenty-five pounds of baggage free. It was during the staging days that Abraham Lincoln visited Atchison and talked to the drivers at the old Massasoit House. Atchison was also the headquarters of a great overland freighting firm, half a dozen steamboats frequently being tied up at its levee at the same time.

When in 1859 Horace Greeley crossed the plains in a stagecoach from Atchison to Denver, he encountered in the upper Solomon Valley a herd of buffalo which reached to the horizon on all sides. He estimated that 512,000 were in sight at one time.

Ben Holladay inaugurated the "Overland Stage Line," with more than one hundred Concord coaches and nearly three thousand horses and mules to draw them. For the eighteen days' journey from Omaha to Sacramento he charged $225. The stages were built in elegant style and each was arranged to carry eight passengers. The mail was guarded by eight men, so armed as to be equal to a small army and ever ready for offensive or defensive warfare with the savages. The bodies of the coaches were beautifully painted, and made water-tight, with the expectation of their being used as boats in ferrying streams. Deep ruts cut by the lumbering Concord coaches are said to be distinctly traceable today three miles east of Great Bend.

The Pony Express followed, covering the two thousand miles over the Oregon Trail in the remarkable time of ten days. During the entire service, but a single bag of mail was lost. Marysville was a home station on the Pony Express route and the original barn still stands in the downtown district, serving as a produce house.

There were 190 stations on the route of the Pony Express, located about ten or twelve miles apart. Upon his arrival at a station the rider found his change of mount ready. He quickly transferred his mail sack to the fresh horse and was soon on his way. The horses were the fleetest mounts the company could procure, well groomed and cared for, and could easily outdistance the horses of the Indians.

The patrons of the Pony Express were chiefly commercial houses, newspapers and the government. The charges were at first five dollars for each half-ounce letter, and communicatons were written on the thinnest procurable tissue, rolled into pencil rolls to economize on space and wrapped in oil-skin for protection against moisture.

President Buchanan's farewell address was carried through in seven days and nineteen hours. The world's record for speed by means of men and horses was established when the text of Lincoln's inaugural address was carried through in seven days and seventeen hours. The service of the Pony Express left behind it a record unsurpassed for enterprise, romance and adventure.

The riders were young men selected for light weight, nerve and general fitness. They received four hundred dollars a year and maintenance. They had no regular uniform, but usually wore buckskin hunting shirts, cloth trousers tucked into high boots, and jockey cap or slouch hat.

In October, 1861, when the telegraph lines from California and Omaha were joined at Salt Lake City, the Pony Express passed into history.

In April, 1935, Elwood and Doniphan county observed the seventy-fifth anniversary of the coming of the first "iron horse" to Kansas. The first train to travel the steel rails in Kansas steamed along a few miles of the Elwood and Marysville Railroad, a section of the contemplated Great Pacific line, on April 24, 1860. Pioneer residents of the territory gathered from near and far and cheered lustily as the engine, "the Albany," huffed and puffed along the tracks. The line was not completed to Troy until after the Civil War. The Albany was borrowed from the Hannibal and St. Joseph, which until 1865 was the only railway spanning Missouri. The locomotive was ferried back across the river. Farmers sometimes hitched oxen to the flat cars to haul wood, but finally the ties rotted and cottonwood sprouts sprang up between the rails.

Then came the great Union Pacific Railway, known at first as the Kansas Pacific, constructed under such difficulties as road builders had never encountered before. There were Indians on every side. The railway workmen had to be expert with the rifle and often a gang was transformed from track-layers into companies of infantry within a few minutes.

The Atchison, Topeka and Santa Fe Railroad entered the valley of the upper Arkansas in 1872, and on the ninth of February, 1880, the first train over that road arrived at Santa Fe, closing forever the Old Santa Fe Trail as a route of commerce.

One of our modern Kansas motor trails is the Victory Highway, a transcontinental highway reaching from New York to San Francisco, and dedicated as a national memorial to the men and women who served the country during the World War. The Victory Highway memorial marker is a figure of an American eagle poised above its nest and young, with outspread wings in an attitude of protection, signifying the protection which this country gives its people. It was developed under the advice of two of America's leading ornithologists, Dr. Theodore Roberts of the University of Minnesota, and Otto Widman of St. Louis, Missouri. It is said to be ornithologically correct in every detail, and possibly the finest American eagle bronze in the United States. It has been designated "The Victory Eagle" and is protected from misuse by copyright. In wing-spread the Victory eagle marker is five and one-half feet; four feet high, with a seven-foot base, and a total height of approximately eleven feet. The markers are being placed on the county lines along the highway.

TAVERN ON OLD SANTA FE TRAIL
Near Burlingame

RUINS OF HOSTELRY
Near Burlingame

42

*I*N THE DAYS when the lumbering Concord coaches crossed the plains from Independence to Santa Fe, stations were built at intervals varying from ten to fifty miles or more. There the animals and drivers were changed and meals furnished to travelers.

Burlingame was one of the most important places on the Santa Fe Trail. An old stone house used as a tavern during those days still stands at the foot of Santa Fe Avenue, while five miles west is a stone inn and distillery, now being used as a barn. This inn, built about 1856, was part of a little settlement, known as Havanna, started by Germans from St. Louis. Just south of the inn was a hostelry with stables for horses and sleeping rooms for travelers. It was two stories high and built with an ell. This structure was burned about fifteen years ago and only one wall remains with the arched doorway through which coaches are said to have been driven.

The building of the American Telephone Company occupies the site of an old blacksmith shop in Burlingame where thousands of horses and oxen were shod for the overland journey to New Mexico.

The oldest blacksmith shop in Kansas is said to be that owned by C. C. Newman in Valley Falls. It has been in continuous operation for seventy years and the original forges, vise and anvils still give good service. A modern trip-hammer was added to the equipment seven years ago. V. P. Newman, the builder of the shop and father of the present owner, was skillful in making horse-shoe nails and in shoeing oxen. Two pairs of antlers adorning the front corners of the roof are relics of pioneer days when elk roamed the region around Ozawkie. A painted sign swinging above the front door reads: "General Black-smithing, Horse Shoeing, Wagon Work." How Mr. Newman finds enough work of this kind to support a family of six children in this day of automobiles is something of a mystery.

A few miles east of Topeka on Victory Highway is a stone dwelling which was built for the accommodation of early pioneers. Because of the fine spring of cold water on the eastern bank of Deer Creek, the place became a favorite camping ground with the prairie schooner tourists of territorial days. One of the most conspicuous features is the giant oak tree towering above the house, its roots strongly held in the bank of the creek.

Near Leavenworth on Highway 73 is a barn standing upon the old

BLACKSMITH SHOP
Valley Falls

STOPPING PLACE FOR STAGES
On Banks of Deer Creek

44

foundation of a tavern built and operated by the mother of Buffalo Bill, after his father, an abolitionist, had been killed by border ruffians. Just beyond this is Cody Hill, so called because on its top, Isaac Cody, the father, built his first house of logs. And it is near here that one can still see the ruts worn by wagon wheels following the Oregon Trail.

Since wagon trains coming out of Leavenworth would generally make their first camp at the foot of this hill, it was a favorable place for Mrs. Cody to build her tavern which she called, "The Valley Grove House." About that time her son, William, became a Pony Express rider, although he was only fifteen years old, the youngest rider on the route.

The tavern was originally a two-storied house — the lower part of stone and the upper part of wood. The frame burned down but a movement is now under way to reconstruct the building as it was and have it marked as the "boyhood home of Buffalo Bill."

We are told that Buffalo Bill earned his nickname while employed as hunter for the construction company of the Kansas Pacific Railroad in 1867-8, when he killed nearly five thousand buffalo to be consumed by the twelve hundred men employed in laying the track.

The Free State Hotel in Lawrence, erected by the New England Emigrant Aid Company in 1855, was probably the best building in the territory, according to Dr. Richard Cordley, who came to Lawrence in 1857 as pastor of the Plymouth Congregational Church.

In his history of Lawrence, Dr. Cordley wrote: "The great lack of Lawrence had been a good hotel. People were hindered from coming to Kansas because they could not be comfortably cared for when they got here. Now they could tell the comfort-loving emigrant that Lawrence had as good a hotel as he could find in St. Louis. He could find a roof and a room the day he arrived, and need not live out-of-doors till he could build a cabin. It was bound to prove an effective element in drawing free-state men to Kansas. The proslavery element felt that to destroy this hotel was to remove a powerful attraction. On May 21, 1856, it was burned to the ground by Sheriff Jones of the proslavery band or posse. This was called the 'sack of Lawrence'."

After the destruction of the hotel, nothing was done toward rebuilding for a year. In the spring of 1857 Colonel S. W. Eldridge and his brother began the erection of another house on the same site. It was of brick, four stories high, and elegantly furnished. The Eldridge House, as it was called, was destroyed in 1863 when Quantrill

PLANTERS' HOUSE
Leavenworth

BUFFALO BILL TAVERN
Near Leavenworth

raided Lawrence and massacred many of its inhabitants. A second Eldridge House was reconstructed immediately; this was razed in 1925 to make room for the present modern, fireproof structure.

One of the most historic old hostelries left in Kansas is the Planters' House in Leavenworth, built in 1855 to accommodate Southern gentry. It became a popular stopping place for the proslavery party in the territory and no known free-soilers were admitted as guests until 1857. At the Leavenworth Hotel built previously on the northwest corner of Main and Delaware streets, free-state men were entertained. This was also known as the Abolition Hotel.

In 1857 the Planters' House was sold to two free-soilers, Len T. Smith and Jep Rice, whose policy was to entertain anyone who paid his bill and acted like a gentleman. They ran the hotel for seven years and had many notable guests. It was the finest hostelry west of St. Louis and afforded from its wide porches a superb view of Platte County's wooded hills across the river. For the past twenty-five years it has been run as an apartment house.

Stephen A. Douglas made his Kansas territorial speech from the balcony of the Planters' House. General William T. Sherman stopped there while in Leavenworth, practicing law for a few months.

It was in December, 1859, that Abraham Lincoln spent a week in Kansas and made six speeches in support of a free-state program. The new railroad across Missouri from Hannibal to St. Joseph had been finished that year and Lincoln came over that road. There were as yet no railroads in Kansas, the first being laid the following year from the river bank at Elwood five miles across the bottoms to Wathena. It was called the St. Joseph and Denver City Railway.

Lincoln spoke at Elwood, Troy, Doniphan and Atchison. Then he drove to Leavenworth and put up at the Planters' House, speaking that night at Stockton's Hall. These speeches first drew attention to Lincoln as a possible president.

Sitting in the audience in Leavenworth was Elisabeth Gertrude Robertson (later Mrs. Ward Burlingame), the first woman in Kansas to receive a teacher's certificate to teach in the public schools. She attended the meeting with her father and after it was concluded was waiting for him to go up and shake hands with Lincoln, when Lincoln noticed her, waved his arms and called, "Let the little miss come up, too."

Later Lincoln was taken across the street to an upstairs room occu-

47

pied by Daniel R. Anthony and others. Dan Anthony wrote of the experience forty years later:

"Lincoln sat there for three hours, his great feet against the stove, his long, lean, ungainly form scrooched down in his tilted-back chair. His reputation as a story-teller is deserved, for he was the leader in swapping tales that night."

This building in which Lincoln spent the evening has been used for many purposes. It housed the first bank established on Kansas soil, and later served as an organ factory, office building, livery and storage barn, saloon and finally the home of a manufacturing concern.

Lincoln spoke again in Leavenworth the following night, December 5. The crowd that gathered was so great that no room nor hall could hold it, and the people massed in the open street in front of the Planters' House. In spite of the intense cold, Lincoln stood for one hour, bareheaded, and spoke from the broad top stone of several steps that led up to the hotel entrance.

When the old Planters' Hotel was remodeled, Senator Stillings carried away the stone steps from which Lincoln spoke that night and set them up at a corner of his farm near Leavenworth.

48

*T*RAVELERS CROSSING western Kansas may see here and there, on the wind-swept plains, little square mounds of earth, hardly more than knots on the landscape. They served as homes for the pioneer home-steaders. In early days when wood could be obtained only with diffi-culty, there were more sod houses than any other kind. Some were built against the sides of hillocks affording protection from gales and cyclones. Others were partly caves or dugouts. Clumps of pig-weed grew about the door. Today it is the boast of many a successful man that he was born in a "soddy," and that his early education was had in a sod schoolhouse. Thurlow Lieurance, composer of Indian music, spent his childhood in a sod house near Pawnee Rock. This house is still standing and doing service as a chicken shelter. As one eastern editor has said, the sod house "was the right stuff for a sturdy pioneer country, and fit for any great man to be born in."

The greensward turned up by the plow was so matted together with the many-rooted buffalo grass as to form better bricks than the Hebrews turned out for Pharaoh, we are told. Cottonwood trees from nearby streams provided rafters. The roof was shingled with other sods which grew green under the spring rains. These crude one or two-roomed shelters had the advantage of being warm in winter and cool in summer. The walls were two or three feet thick.

Most of the houses were not papered inside, but when they were it was usually with newspapers. One man who was reared in a soddy recollects that his father was wont to read those papers on the wall. His wife, in order to break him of the habit, repapered the walls one day when father was out plowing. Although she had to use newspapers again, she put them on upside down.

A sod house has many enemies that work to wear down its walls. Field-mice honeycomb them with their burrows. Rain and snow tear at the earthen walls and winds shake them. Yet without upkeep the average life of a sod house is thirty-five or forty years. As late as 1929 a printed report of the Kansas School Code Commission contained cuts of sod school houses still being used in western counties.

Perhaps the sole surviving soddy in Stafford County is that on the Henry Volker homestead, ten miles northeast of Stafford. Some county residents insist that it has weathered the Kansas climate for fifty-seven years. The wall is badly shaled away outside, but is as good as ever within. The sod was hauled from the Ninnescah valley,

Sod Houses

SOD HOUSE
Logan County

SOD SCHOOLHOUSE
Scott County

50

miles away, according to pioneers who saw houses rise from the plains in early days. The marshy turf was cut in long strips, rolled into bundles, and hauled to the site where the strips were laid, basket-weave style, to build the walls.

The last wild buffalo known to have been in Stafford County was seen in the spring of 1879. Two small boys, Harve and Perry Crawford, now prominent Stafford residents, came running into the house, breathless with excitement, to tell their mother that a sod house was coming up over the hill southwest of town. The sod house proved to be a great shaggy buffalo. The animal plodded on up into the little frontier town but stayed only a few minutes, galloping off into the sand hills. The father of the boys with another plainsman followed the beast and shot it, bringing their heavy burden home in triumph.

Many years ago modernized communities of the western prairies began to shake their heads at the "little old sod shanty on the claim" and chambers of commerce started campaigns to have them torn down on the theory that they were a bad advertisement of a community. Counties boasted when their last little mud-colored cabin was destroyed and proclaimed the news abroad.

A dispatch from Salina was printed in papers throughout the country in 1920 stating: "This is the year of the passing of the sod house in Western Kansas. Except those kept as souvenirs of the early days, and through sentiment, there will be scarcely any of them left after this fall. In the years of figuring and worrying to make both ends meet the farmer of Western Kansas was content to live in a soddy. But now prosperity is here and the sod house has passed with the poverty of former years."

When the Civilian Conservation Corps went out to build a dam near Dodge City in 1933, the engineers were confronted with the problem of a suitable material to use in building houses to shelter the six hundred workmen. Someone suggested a cantonment of sod houses and advertisements were put in county newspapers asking for expert advice on their construction. As a result scores of letters were received from old-timers experienced in making sod houses, some of them from women. Sixty men came across the plains from various points in Kansas and adjoining states and were put to work at once. Ten sod buildings were completed, their greater dimensions necessitating side walls much thicker than those of the little shanties of former days. Nine similar structures were put up to accommodate CCC boys at the Sheridan state lake near Quinter.

POTTAWATOMIE BAPTIST MISSION
Near Topeka

SHAWNEE MISSION
Near Kansas City

CALIFORNIA has usually been regarded as the "Mission State," and her fourteen or fifteen missions constitute one of her chief attractions. Kansas also was once well equipped with missions. During the '40s and '50s about thirty were established by various denominations. Some are still maintained, but the majority have faded away, or serve as cattle barns or machinery sheds.

The Kansas legislature has adopted measures for the preservation of some of these old landmarks, among them Shawnee Mission in Johnson County. At this point the Methodist Episcopal Church established in 1839 a little Indian mission which had been started in 1830 at a landing on the Kansas River, now known as Turner. The United States government was induced to allot two thousand, two hundred and forty acres of land besides giving regular financial aid.

The Reverend Thomas Johnson was placed in charge of the mission, which was known as the Shawnee Indian Manual Labor School. It was the first effort of the government to fit the Indian for citizenship by manual training. Students came from as many as ten tribes, including the Pawnee, Cheyenne, Sioux, Wyandotte, Delaware, Pottawatomie, Shawnee and others. For many years one hundred students or more were educated and housed here during each school session.

As the school developed it became a typical village in itself. In all, there were some sixteen buildings, in addition to tool shops, a blacksmith shop, a sawmill and a grist mill, a brick yard and trade shops, The lumber was cut and sawed from the trees in the timber along the nearby creek and made by hand into window frames, door sashes, etc. Even now the marks of the adz can be seen on the hand-hewn rafters and lathings. Between the main building, the mission proper, and a big brick dormitory ran the old Santa Fe Trail.

The first orchard in Kansas was started when Mr. Johnson planted twelve acres in apple trees. A crop report from the fields for the first year showed many bushels of wheat, oats, corn and potatoes. The livestock included cattle, hogs, work horses and three buffalo.

The mission was first used for civil purposes in 1855, when it housed the territorial legislature with Andrew H. Reeder as the first territorial executive. During the Civil War the buildings were barracks of Union troops, and before and after the war formed headquarters for Indian campaigns, affording protection to the settlers. The school had been finally abandoned in 1864.

Through the efforts of the Shawnee Mission Association, the D. A. R., and the Colonial Dames, the legislature in 1927 was induced to purchase what remained of the mission then belonging to four different individuals. Three of the original buildings stand as staunchly as on the day when erected and are being restored to their former dignity and beauty by the Kansas State Historical Society. Rooms in the main building have been assigned to various patriotic organizations, which make annual pilgrimages to this historic old landmark.

On a tract of ten acres in Johnson County is the site of the first Baptist Mission in Kansas. In 1830 the subject of establishing this mission was considered in an interview with a Shawnee council, consisting of twenty chiefs, and during 1832 the mission house and other buildings were erected.

Here the following year Jotham Meeker installed the first printing press that was brought into the territory. It was used extensively for publications in English and in the languages of several Indian tribes. Primers, booklets and translations were published in the Shawnee, Creek, Choctaw, Otoe, Pottawatomie, Wea, Delaware, Osage and Kansas languages. Other missions used some of these books in their work.

About this time Meeker commenced publication of a small periodical called the "Shawnoe Sun," the first newspaper ever published entirely in the Indian language, as well as the first newspaper ever published in Kansas. It was continued by Johnson Lykins, another missionary.

Out of the Baptist Ottawa Mission grew indirectly Ottawa University. This mission was established in 1837 by Reverend Jotham Meeker. He brought his printing press from the Shawnee Baptist Mission in 1849 to print books and translations of the New Testament for the Ottawa Indians.

The Pottawatomie Baptist Mission, established in 1848, was located five miles west of Topeka. It served as a manual labor school and had thirty children in daily attendance. The Pottawatomie tribe in 1862 moved westward, abandoning the school.

Serving now as a stable, the main building of this group still stands. A bronze marker was erected by the Topeka chapter of the D. A. R. in 1932 designating the site of the mission. The old stone building, one of the first erected in Shawnee County, consisted of twelve rooms. It had two cross walls of stone three stories high. The walls of the first story were two feet thick and those above, one and a half feet.

One of the territorial governors, John W. Geary, while stopping at this mission for a few days, wrote and signed a Thanksgiving proclamation, the second issued in Kansas. The mission was a regular stopping point on the route west. There was a ferry across the Kansas River about a mile and a half north of the present building on the way to Fort Riley.

The town of St. Paul in Neosho County was known as Osage Mission until 1894. The Osages came from Missouri early in the nineteenth century and withdrew from Kansas into the Indian Territory, that is now Oklahoma, in 1870. This mission was established in 1847.

The first settlement at St. Mary's was made by the Pottawatomie Indians in 1848, who were moved there under the direction of Kansas Catholic missionaries. St. Mary's College was built in the same location selected for the erection of the first rude shelters.

A Quaker mission was established in 1834 near Merriam. It was supported by the Society of Friends in Ohio and Indiana. The mission property comprised two hundred acres of land under cultivation. The building was a large frame house, all of solid walnut timber. Each board and beam was hand-sawed and the nails were hand-forged. There was a huge fireplace for cooking. Through the basement floor water was drawn up from a well. A row of honey locusts and cedars grew along the front of the house and in the rear was an apple orchard.

Upon entering the mission, the Indian children were obliged to have their hair cut. They were then bathed, given clothes, and taught how to put them on and off. Each child was equipped with a queer little Quaker hat or bonnet and given an English name. One thousand Shawnee Indians lived on this reservation. The mission was abandoned about the beginning of the Civil War and the land sold to different persons. In 1923 the Olathe chapter of the D. A. R. placed a red granite boulder on the site to preserve its memory.

Part of the walls of the Iowa, Sac and Fox Mission near Highland still stands and a plan is under way among former Highland College students to restore the building. About 1834 the Iowa and Sac Indians made treaties ceding land to the Board of Home Missions of the Presbyterian Church. On this land in Doniphan County Reverend S. M. Irvin built the Iowa, Sac and Fox Mission in 1845. It was a three-story building containing thirty-two rooms, a chapel and a dining hall. Here was established the second printing press in Kansas, put

55

PRESBYTERIAN MISSION
Highland

KAW MISSION
Council Grove

into use nine years later than the Meeker press, but eleven years before the first professional paper, the Leavenworth Weekly Herald.

The Kaw Indian Mission, founded in 1850 by Thomas S. Huffaker, was situated on the west bank of the Neosho River. It is now a residence located near the business section of Council Grove. A monument stands in almost the same spot as the belfry tower, from which in years gone by pealed an alarm bell to warn citizens in case of Indian raids or fire. The bell was in use for more than forty years, having been hauled across country from Lawrence by ox-team.

During the Kaw raid on Council Grove in 1859 and the Cheyenne raid on the Kaws in 1868, the women and children of the town were barricaded within the mission, which served as a fortress for the surrounding territory.

About three miles down the Neosho River the government built two other Indian schools, both of which have been torn down. In one of these a quarter-blood Indian boy of Topeka was enrolled for a short time. He was the late Charles Curtis who became Vice-president of the United States. One day when a report came that the Cheyennes were on the war-path, the eight-year-old lad is said to have ridden on his pony sixty or more miles to Topeka to summon aid.

Although the Indians loved Mr. Huffaker and called him "Father" and accepted his decrees without a murmur, they did not take kindly to the school. The daughters of the tribe were not allowed to attend, and the sons of the chiefs and leading men would have felt disgraced if they had received instruction in the white men's school. Consequently it was made up principally of orphans and such Indian children as had no one to care for them. The largest number of students to attend at one time was forty.

There being no school for white children at Council Grove, Mr. Huffaker in May, 1851, organized them into a school and taught them at the mission. Fifteen white children attended. Here, too, was the first Sunday School between Shawnee Mission and Denver.

BUILDING AT FORT LEAVENWORTH
Used for First Territorial Capitol

SHAWNEE MISSION
Near Kansas City

THE LOCATING of the state capital demanded much time and attention on the part of the early settlers. Kansas Territory was opened to settlement on May 30, 1854, by an act of Congress which located the seat of government temporarily at Fort Leavenworth, and provided that the buildings of the fort should be occupied for the public offices. The first territorial governor, Andrew H. Reeder, arrived in the territory, October 4 of the same year, and established his executive office at the fort.

Rooms in a brick building on the west side of the plaza were assigned to the governor for his residence. For his executive office he had a room in the old stone building at the northwest corner of the plaza or parade ground, known and occupied as the quartermaster's department. This was an L-shaped one-story building. It was torn down in 1893 to make room for the edifice known as Pope Hall.

Although Fort Leavenworth has the distinction of having been the first capital of Kansas, it remained such for only fifty days. On November 24, the governor removed his office to the Shawnee Indian Mission, a mile from the Missouri state line. This mission had been established in 1830 by Reverend Thomas Jefferson under the auspices of the Methodist Church.

At the time of the arrival of Governor Reeder, the mission was at its full strength. The accommodations at Fort Leavenworth had proved unsuitable for the executive offices, whereas the mission afforded large and roomy buildings. There were no white settlements in the territory except at Forts Leavenworth, Scott, and Riley, and at the Indian missions and agencies.

The officers were given lounging and office rooms and took their meals at the boarding department of the mission family. The mission consisted of three large brick buildings besides work shops. The three were within one hundred yards of each other in the form of a triangle. At the north was the building for the girls' department. The superintendent and his family also lived here. Another was for the boys and their teachers and contained the mission schoolroom and chapel. On the southwest was the boarding house in which were tables capable of seating two hundred people at a time.

On April 16, 1855, the governor issued a proclamation requesting that the legislature meet at the town of Pawnee on July 2. The following day he himself left the territory on a visit to his family in

FIRST CAPITOL OF KANSAS
Pawnee

CONSTITUTION HALL 1856
Topeka

FIRST CAPITOL
After Restoration

Pennsylvania, and Secretary Daniel Woodson, as acting governor, held office until June 23.

Pawnee was located on the north side of the Kansas River at the eastern line of the Fort Riley military reservation. The town had been projected by Pennsylvania friends of Governor Reeder and others in 1854. The Kansas River was then supposed to be a good navigable stream as far as Fort Riley. River navigation, it was thought, would invite early and large settlements to that interior section of the territory. Railroads had not yet penetrated Kansas Territory.

Honorable Robert Klotz, who had served as a member of congress from Pennsylvania, and who later became a member of the Kansas state legislature, superintended the building of the town and the erection of a capitol. This was a two-story stone structure, 40 by 80 feet in size. It was well provided with seats and writing tables. The lower floor was given to the House, and the Council convened in the second story.

Although ample provisions had been made in the way of boarding houses for the accommodation of the legislators, these arrangements were ignored by the members, who arrived by the water route or in wagons drawn by oxen, by horseback or by foot. They staked their own tents around their own campfires and ate their own bacon and corn bread. When some cows strayed into camp they were quickly corraled by a circle of stalwart men while other legislators tried their hands at milking, with gratifying results.

On July 3, 1855, the governor's message was delivered to the legislature but his wishes were openly ignored. A bill was passed on the following day transferring the seat of government to the Shawnee Mission. Governor Reeder vetoed the bill but it was passed over his veto. The legislature then adjourned to reconvene at Shawnee Mission on July 16.

The stone building at Pawnee housed the first Kansas territorial legislature only four days. For more than fifty years it stood neglected. In 1877 a windstorm tore off the roof, the windows were broken out, and nothing remained except the four gaunt walls. Finally, in 1907, a $500 fund was raised by state-wide subscriptions to repair the walls, and in 1926 the state legislature appropriated $1,000 for the same purpose.

Meanwhile the Union Pacific Railroad had been built, the tracks passing within a few feet of the old building. Railway officials decided to restore it completely to its original state. Huge timbers, fifty

61

EARLY CAPITOL AT LECOMPTON

STANTON'S HOUSE
Near Lecompton

feet in length, were used in the reconstruction, the exposed surfaces being chipped by adzes to imitate hand-hewn lumber. The floors are of two-inch planks with rough finish. Iron nails and dowel pins were used to hold the timbers and lumber together. Hanging lamps were installed, and old benches, stoves and antique furniture were found to help create the atmosphere of early days. The roof alone cost more than $2,000, being made of three-foot shingles, hand-split to imitate "shakes."

On August 2, 1928, the old building was redecorated and memorialized as "Kansas' first territorial capitol." Since that time many individuals have given articles of interest to the historical collection. A custodian is in charge at all times and the building is maintained for inspection by the Kansas State Historical Society.

Lecompton was a stirring place in the spring of 1856. Warrants for the arrest of free-state men concerned in the acts which brought on the Wakarusa War, and for the arrest of many others who had been prominent in the defense of Lawrence, were put in the hands of United States marshals and sheriffs. Early in May Lecompton became a military camp with troops in bivouac, marching and counter-marching in expeditions to put down free-state settlers in their resistance, and to stop outrages of marauding bands of proslavery recruits. If all the incidents occurring there were put upon record, the place would be shown to have been, next to Lawrence, perhaps the focal center of the greatest activity of strife in arms among the settlers in Kansas during the territorial period.

One of the oldest and most interesting mansions in the state is that built in 1857 by Frederick P. Stanton, secretary and acting governor of the territory of Kansas. He was an able, scholarly lawyer who had served ten years in Congress as representative from Tennessee before being appointed to the Kansas Territory by President Buchanan.

Governor Stanton, thinking Lecompton would soon be a flourishing city, chose for his home a site about three miles away which would be "out of the noise and whirl of business." The house, known as Mount Aeolia, stood on a bluff overlooking the river and was much admired by people passing in steamboats. Now it is so surrounded by trees and underbrush on the north as to be difficult to find.

This typically southern mansion is a dignified two-story structure of native stone. It is said to have been planned chiefly by Mrs. Stanton, since her husband was away much of the time. There are seventeen rooms, twelve of which have fireplaces. All of the woodwork is walnut; which although very simple in design, varies a little in the different rooms. There are stories of fabulous prices offered by the government for the woodwork during the last war.

Governor Stanton brought many negro servants to Lecompton and in early days southern hospitality reigned within the walls. Dancing and merry-making made the place a center of social life and it was noted for the splendor that went with it. During the period of the Civil War this house was a refuge for people for miles around.

The second territorial legislature convened at Lecompton, January 12, 1857, and adjourned, February 20. During that spring the immigration to Kansas was immense — almost wholly from the northern states. The free-state party in the fall elected a majority of the legislature. The third territorial and free-state legislature met in Lecompton, December 7, 1857, in extra session, adjourned and met again, January 4, 1858. On the next day, by joint action of the two branches, an adjournment was made to Lawrence where the legislature met, January 8, and held a session, adjourning finally February 13.

Lawrence now became practically the capital of the territory, for free-state conventions had met there often before, and this had been the focus of free-state agitation and sentiment. The place had often been threatened and once sacked. On the adjournment to Lawrence, the governor removed his office there during the sitting of the legislature.

Minneola missed becoming the capital of Kansas by only a hair's breadth. Under the leadership of Perry Fuller, a scheme was evolved to start a capital in Franklin County. The stock-holders included almost every prominent leader in the free-state cause. Among the buildings erected were a hotel, a governor's mansion and a large hall to be used for legislative purposes. In 1858 the legislature passed a bill making Minneola the capital, but the bill was vetoed by Governor Denver. An appeal was taken to the United States attorney-general, who decided the bill was void. Before his decision many other buildings went up and the town had a population of several hundred. The legislature called the constitutional convention there, and Lane was elected chairman. A motion was made to adjourn to Leavenworth, and after a debate lasting a day and a night, the motion carried. This sealed the fate of Minneola and today the former town-site boasts only a half-dozen farms and has nothing to show for its day of glory.

Then followed more moving back and forth between Lecompton and Lawrence. As early as 1855 the free-state party in Kansas had named Topeka as the capital of the state, and it became the capital under the free-state constitutional movement. At a constitutional convention held in Topeka a vote was taken resulting in twenty votes for Topeka and sixteen for Lawrence as the capital.

At that time there were but a few scattered buildings in Topeka. The building at 425 Kansas Avenue, which became known as Constitution Hall, was the most substantial. Here five meetings of the Topeka free-state legislature were held, and so the way was paved for the permanent location of the capital.

A convention known as the Wyandotte Constitutional Convention was held in July, 1859. It provided that Topeka should be the temporary capital and that the legislature should submit the question of the permanent location to a vote of the people. The first state legislature under the Wyandotte constitution met in Topeka, March 26, 1861. There were scant accommodations for the sitting of the state legislature and for the offices of the state. There were not more than eight hundred inhabitants in the town.

Governor Robinson rented rooms for the executive offices in the Ritchie block at the corner of Sixth Street and Kansas Avenue. In the third story of this building the Senate met, and for three years it held its sessions there. The first House of Representatives met in the Gale block. Late in the session, owing to a leaking roof, the members of the House went over and sat in the Congregational Church at the corner of Seventh and Harrison Streets. In 1863 it met in the Methodist Church. The same year the state agreed to rent for a time a building which should be erected for state uses. It was built on Kansas Avenue, taking in part of the old Constitution Hall. In this building the legislature of 1864 sat, and it continued to be the home of the legislature and state offices until the east wing of the present capitol came to be occupied in 1869.

It was in 1862 that Cyrus K. Holliday, president of the Topeka Association, formally conveyed a tract of land to the state for a capitol building, and his gift was accepted by the legislature. In 1866 the legislature provided for the erection of the east wing of the capitol. On the 17th of October the corner-stone was laid. The wing was occupied by the state offices in December, 1869. Further appropriations were made from time to time until the entire building was completed in 1903. The total cost was $3,200,588.92. The extreme diameter or breadth of the building, including the porches, north and south, is 399 feet; east and west, 385 feet; the square of the dome at the base is 80 by 80 feet; the height of the dome to the extreme top is 304 feet.

The original plans called for the erection of a statue of Ceres, the goddess of agriculture, on top of the dome. The executive council, however, declined to spend the necessary $6,950 for the statue. The Ceres would have weighed five tons. There was considerable talk in regard to the statue, some people declaring that as agriculture was not the only industry in the state, it would be well to have a statue made which would represent the schools and churches. Others suggested the erection of statues of Charles Robinson, Jim Lane, or of Indians or buffalo. No agreement was reached and the matter was indefinitely postponed.

STATE CAPITOL
Topeka

PROBABLY THE VERY OLDEST Protestant church west of the Missouri River was the Highland Presbyterian Church, organized at the Iowa Indian Mission, October 21, 1843. The first member received, except by transfer, was an Indian girl. In Wilder's "Annals of Kansas," we read: "The first minister of the Presbyterian Church who settled in Kansas was Reverend S. M. Irvin. He was appointed by the Foreign Board to superintend the Iowa Mission, near what is now Highland in Doniphan County. That was in 1835."

After Irvin Hall on the Highland College campus was completed in 1859, and until 1885, this building served as the "chapel" for services of the Presbyterian Church. Afterwards an attractive edifice was erected across the street from the college.

The first church in Kansas to be built by a congregation that expected to worship in it was that erected by the Wyandotte Indians in Kansas City in 1844. They were members of the Methodist Episcopal Church, who brought their organization with them when they came from Ohio to Kansas. The church stood in the vicinity of Eighteenth and Washington Streets, three miles from the junction of the Missouri and Kansas Rivers. The building was of hewn logs with a clapboard roof and puncheons for floor and seats. Esquire Grey Eyes, the ordained local preacher, was instrumental in erecting the structure, even before he built a residence for himself. The first meeting was held in the latter part of April. Reverend James Wheeler, a missionary, came to work with the Indians the following month.

This original building was used until 1847 when it was replaced by a brick church on a tract near Tenth and Walker Streets, and no further mention can be found of the first building after that date.

The division of the Methodist Church in 1844 on the subject of slavery brought much trouble to the Wyandottes, causing them to split. After 1849 two branches were maintained. The Church South kept possession of the brick edifice, while the Northern branch held services in a vacant house and in a grove until a log building was completed near the Quindaro cemetery. Feeling was bitter, however, and on April 8, 1856, both churches were burned. They were rebuilt and continue to this day. Each claims to be the true descendant of the congregation that built the first church under the direction of Squire Grey Eyes.

TRINITY CHAPEL
Lawrence

EMMANUEL CHURCH
Near Topeka

68

It is generally conceded that the first church for white settlers in Kansas was the Plymouth Congregational erected at Lawrence in 1854. Within ten weeks after the arrival of the first pioneer in Lawrence this church was organized by S. Y. Lum, a Congregational minister.

To the parish of St. Paul's, Leavenworth, belongs the honor of being the first organized Episcopal parish and of having built the first Episcopal Church in the territory in 1856. The building was a small wooden edifice in which services were held for several years, until the Church of St. Paul was built.

Trinity Parish in Lawrence was organized in 1858. The following year a small stone building resembling a country school house on the prairie was built and consecrated by Bishop Kemper. Two months after Quantrill's raid Dr. Robert Oliver became the rector. He began immediately to transform the homely little building into the beautiful one of the present day, adding a new chancel in its proper place in the east, a tower, vestibule, diamond panel windows and a transept. This was completed in 1865. He built the rectory and secured lots for the larger church. The cloisters were added in 1931. Dr. Oliver was the first chancellor of the University of Kansas. Trinity Chapel is the oldest Episcopal Church now standing in the state.

Twelve miles southeast of Topeka in Monmouth township is an old stone church which was built in 1871. The walls of the structure, now overgrown with ivy, are about to collapse and the glass in the Gothic windows has entirely disappeared. Tipping at a precarious angle is the old wooden belfry, perched on a broken stone foundation at the gable of the roof.

Emmanuel Church, as it was called, was always a mission church. It was abandoned about twenty-five years ago. Dr. J. N. Lee, the rector of Grace Church in Topeka, organized the mission work in Monmouth township and was largely instrumental in securing the building. He started services there soon after coming to Topeka.

A short distance from Ottawa stand the picturesque ruins of another Episcopal Church, once beloved and dear to the ideals of early settlers in that part of the country. It is worth a ride of many miles to view the crimson and orange of a sunset framed by this graceful Gothic arch. Vines cling lovingly to the old gray stone.

On December 2, 1859, the day John Brown was executed at Charleston, Abraham Lincoln came to Atchison and spoke on "The Issue of the Day" in the Methodist Church, which then stood on the hill at the corner of Fifth and Parallel Streets. During the early days

69

RUINS OF UNITED
BRETHREN CHURCH
Big Springs

CONGREGATIONAL CHURCH
Wabaunsee

of the Civil War this was the first church in Atchison to have the Stars and Stripes raised over it.

The old Congregational Church in Wabaunsee stands as it did more than three-quarters of a century ago, a reminder of the Puritan ideals of its builders and a fitting memorial to Henry Ward Beecher. It was built in 1862 by the Beecher Bible and Rifle Colony which came to Kansas in 1856 as a result of the great agitation in New England over the Kansas-Nebraska bill. Wabaunsee, an Indian name meaning "early dawn," was one of the first towns founded in the interest of the free-state movement. The site was selected by five advance guards from New Haven, Connecticut, sent to choose a location.

When ardent anti-slavery followers had gathered in the North Church in New Haven to enroll men to go to the new territory and fight for freedom, Henry Ward Beecher gave a stirring address. President Benjamin Silliman, of Yale University, made the suggestion that each man be equipped with a Sharp rifle and Beecher seconded the motion. From his pulpit in Brooklyn, New York, Henry Ward Beecher made the following statement:

"I believe the Sharp rifle to be a truly moral agency and that there is more moral power in one of these instruments, so far as the slaveholders of Kansas are concerned, than in a hundred Bibles. You might as well read the Bible to buffaloes as to those fellows who follow Atchison and Stringfellow."

Thereafter "Beecher's Bibles" were understood to mean the Sharp rifles. When a group of New Englanders were on their way to Kansas by wagon with a consignment of rifles and ammunition, they were asked by Missourians, "What are you loaded with?"

"Beecher's Bibles for the Indians," was the reply that let them pass unmolested through the proslavery lines.

After the colonists arrived at Wabaunsee they began immediately the founding of what was to be "the New Haven of the West." The cabins that were built became stations on the underground railway which operated in aiding runaway slaves to escape. The Sharp rifles soon came into active use. A military company, the Prairie Guards, was organized under the leadership of Captain William Mitchell, and in September of 1856 went to Lawrence to help protect the town against proslavery fighters.

Richard Cordley writes in the Kansas Annual Register, "It is doubtful whether any western colony ever contained so large a propor-

METHODIST CHURCH
Lawrence

BELL FROM EARLY UNITARIAN CHURCH
Lawrence

tion of thoroughly educated Christian men, as this colony at Wabaunsee."

According to Charles B. Lines, a deacon in the New Haven Church and president of the colony, two of the charter members of the Beecher Rifles Church were women.

"They left the walls of their own homes unplastered that the walls of their church be not bare," Lines commented in a letter written to the New York Sun in 1856.

The attendance steadily increased until in 1861 this church reported the largest membership of any in Kansas. The Reverend Harry Jones was the first minister. The building still stands but is no longer used for church services.

"The Stone Church" west of Maple Hill, built and dedicated in 1885, is another picturesque structure erected by Congregationalists. It, too, is now used only on special occasions.

In 1856 the first United Brethren Church in the state was erected at Big Springs by Rev. W. A. Cardwell, a staunch free-stater and a foe of the liquor traffic. Much early history revolves around the Big Springs community, and the United Brethren Church there played an important part in those stirring days. The ruins still remain on the south side of Highway 40, across from the new building and parsonage.

Many churches suffered because of the Quantrill raid, among them those at Lawrence, Osawatomie, and Wakarusa, but, as someone has said, "they rose again in the strength of Christian heroism and pushed the work with renewed vigor."

The financial loss to the Lawrence Plymouth Church was great but in a few months it recovered and was able to get along without outside aid. The site of the first Methodist Church in Lawrence has been marked as a historic spot. The ground was purchased, July 6, 1855, a building was erected two years later, and after the Quantrill raid August 21, 1863, it was used as a morgue. The frame building still stands near the office of the Telephone Company on Vermont Street.

Lawrence claims the first Unitarian Church in Kansas. It was erected during the early days of border warfare at the foot of old North College Hill. It was begun in 1856, but more than once threatened invasion stopped work upon it, and on one occasion when about half done, its walls served as a fort. It was already in use in 1857, although not completed until two years later.

Funds for the erection of this building came largely from friends in

Boston interested in the free-state movement as much as in the liberal church. In the minutes of the first meeting, Feb. 3, 1856, is a statement that "between three and four thousand dollars has been pledged at the East and one thousand here . . . ."

Records show that the thermometer that year from early December to the first of March hovered around zero and for nearly three weeks wavered between ten and thirty degrees below with much high wind and a heavy fall of snow, but the weather deterred the builders little more than did the border warfare.

This being the first public gathering place in Lawrence, the building, when finally finished, served many purposes. At least one other church formed its society within the Unitarian walls. Not only did the first free school in the state find shelter in the building, but also the first high school, known as the Quincy High School, and the first university, called Lawrence University.

In the roll of the school as of the church are many of the prominent names of early Lawrence history. The school drew from the entire community and the church from all the folks of liberal religious intent. Signers of the first church books, included Governor and Mrs. Charles Robinson, Mr. and Mrs. B. W. Woodward, G. W. Hutchinson, Abram Wilder, J. W. Wilder, James Blood, Geo. W. Goss, and others. Later years brought such outstanding figures as Alfred Whitman, Miss Sarah Brown, Mrs. Sarah Stone, Hervey White, and William Herbert Carruth.

Distinguished speakers aside from the ministers who occupied the pulpit included Robert Collyer, Ralph Waldo Emerson, Edward Everett Hale, John Pierrepoint, Lucy Stone, Julia Ward Howe, Henry Blackwell, and Dr. William G. Eliot.

During the ministry of Dr. C. G. Howland, a new church became necessary, and in 1891, the Unitarian Society abandoned the historic old church for its present building. The original bell still remains, however, and is mounted in the Junior High School belfry where it can be heard on special occasions. The metal for it was contributed by women of Massachusetts.

$\mathcal{B}$AKER UNIVERSITY at Baldwin claims to be the oldest living college in Kansas whose service has been continuous since its charter was granted, February 12, 1858. While other charters were given educational bodies about that date, Baker is the only institution that has maintained a four-year course during the intervening years.

It was in Kibbey Cabin, formerly located on the highest promontory in the region of Palmyra, that Dr. W. H. Goode preached the first sermon to the white settlers of the Kansas-Nebraska Territory. Here, a meeting of the educational convention of the Methodist Episcopal Church was called on March 18, 1857, to consider proposals relative to founding a university in one of the following towns: Blue Mound, Prairie City, Centropolis, Lawrence, and Topeka.

An offer made by the Palmyra township association of 640 acres of land was considered perhaps the deciding factor in locating the new educational institution at Baldwin. It was named Baker in honor of Bishop Osman C. Baker, president of the first session of the Kansas-Nebraska conference. He gave the college a three-hundred-pound bell which for many years hung in the belfry of Old Science Hall and was used as a curfew not only for the college but for the town. At the time of the death of Abraham Lincoln, the bell tolled twenty-four consecutive hours. It is now mounted on a pedestal on the south campus.

For many years no buildings were placed on the Baker campus because of lack of funds to erect such an ideal building as the trustees deemed worthy to grace such splendid grounds. For this reason the first college building of stone, two stories high, was erected one block east of the campus. Built in 1858, the "Old Castle," as it was called, is said to be the oldest college building in Kansas.

In the "Annals of Baker University," 1917, we read: "The college building was the center of influence and activity and the value of lots was determined by their proximity to it. It was at once the college, the church, the town hall and the lyceum. Here were held religious revivals, political rallies and school exhibitions. Here met the old Philopenthian Society, the herald in Kansas of equal rights and privileges between the sexes, and here boys and girls stood side by side upon the same platform and contended for oratorical honors without prejudice. Its walls could tell stories that would be poems and in it the

OLD CASTLE
Baldwin

OLD SCIENCE HALL
Baker University

76

antiquary would be in touch with the beginnings of Kansas civilization.''

A short time after the college opened, a farmer came to town with some grain to grind. Dr. Werter R. Davis, the first president, was standing in the front door when the farmer drove up and, thinking the college a mill, asked if he could get his grist ground that day. President Davis informed him that this was the place where they made men, not flour.

The Masons of Baldwin assisted in building another story on the edifice and used that part as a lodge hall for several years.

In 1863 the one building was found insufficient to meet the educational needs of the country and an agent was appointed to travel through the eastern states and solicit subscriptions. Abraham Lincoln, at that time President of the United States, donated one hundred dollars to the young Kansas college to apply on a new building. This is the only contribution of such a nature Lincoln is known to have made. The opening day of the spring term, in March, 1871, was known as "moving up day," when the students carried their seats and tables, desks and books in a long procession from the Old Castle up to new Science Hall on the campus. One story only of the new building was completed at that time and the only furniture in it was that carried in the arms of the students and professors.

For a period of about twenty years the Old Castle was used for a number of purposes — as a home for the president, living quarters for many of the Baker students, and later as a mill. From 1896 until 1909 it stood empty and deteriorated, the title having been in private hands from 1880 until 1909. Then the title was again transferred to the Kansas Educational Association, the name under which Baker University operates.

In 1927 the alumni carried on a financial campaign to restore the building. A considerable amount of money was spent in putting in a new cement floor, a new roof and beams. It is now in a fine state of preservation, being used only for storage.

Old Science Hall, still standing at the north end of the campus, ceased functioning as a classroom building when the science department moved into the new Mulvane Science building in 1925. It still houses one of the finest collections of birds, animals and geological specimens in this section of the country.

This hall was the "batching" quarters of Bishop William Alfred Quayle when he came to Baker University as a student. After his

IRVIN HALL
Highland College

TAUY JONES' HOME
Near Ottawa

78

graduation, while still a young man, he was chosen president of the university. He later became a bishop of the Methodist Church and was well known as a poet, lecturer and essayist. At his death in 1925 his remarkable collection of Bibles went to the university library. Bishop Quayle had obtained many of the rarest printings known, in addition to scrolls and manuscripts which antedate the invention of printing. It is one of the most notable collections of Bibles in the world.

Another school which received its charter at about the same time was Highland College in Doniphan County. This charter was granted to the Highland University Company, February 9, 1858. Reverend S. M. Irvin, a Presbyterian missionary from Pennsylvania, had opened a school for the Iowa, Sac and Fox Indians near the present location of the college in 1837. Twenty years later, when Kansas was opened for settlement, the government moved many of the tribes to the west. Father Irvin devoted the rest of his life to the task of building a school for the white settlers who were then coming to Kansas Territory in large numbers.

The corner-stone of Irvin Hall was laid in 1858 and the building was completed the following year. This brick structure with its picturesque belfry still stands as an important part of the thriving junior college, based upon the Christian ideals of Father Irvin. On the campus a "pioneer rose garden" has been started. One of the most prized specimens is the "Mother Irvin Rose" which was brought to Kansas and planted at the old Indian mission the year it was established.

Ottawa University was established by the combined efforts of white Baptists and the Ottawa Indians. The first movement for such a school came in 1859 when the Baptists of the state, realizing the need of a Christian educational institution, secured a charter to found what they named the Roger Williams University.

John Tecumseh Jones, popularly called "Tauy," a contraction of Ottawa, who had for several years been the interpreter for the Ottawa Indians, and had by them been adopted into the tribe, took an active part in the development and location of the university. Through his leadership the government set apart 20,000 acres of land and the site was selected with the understanding that the school would be available for both Indians and white men. The first building, now known as Tauy Jones Hall, was begun in 1864. The following year the institution took its present name, Ottawa University.

In 1845 Tauy Jones had married Miss Jane Kelly, an accomplished young woman sent out by the Baptist Missionary Society to work among the Indians. They settled on the Woodlief Ranch, six miles northeast of Ottawa. A large stone house was built and is still in use. The stone for it was cut in Fort Scott and hauled from there by ox teams. For many years this served as a mission school where Indian children were taught. The tract of land was never farmed by Tauy Jones himself, but was left to the care of others while he gave himself to the problem of education. It is said that the young university was "the idol of his heart and for it he gave much of means, talent and of prayer."

When the Ottawa Indians were moved to Oklahoma in 1867 a new arrangement was made by which Ottawa University was retained by the white Baptists. A section of land known as "college farm" and 1,280 additional acres were saved for the institution. The town of Ottawa was laid out in the heart of the Ottawa Indian reservation, and through it flows the "Swan-stream" or Marais des Cygnes.

In Governor Crawford's message, January 9, 1866, quoted in Wilder's Annals, the following colleges and universities in Kansas are listed: Baker University at Baldwin, under the control of the Methodist Episcopal Church; Lane University, Douglas County, under the United Brethren Church; Ottumwa College, Coffey County, under the Christian Church; Highland University, Doniphan County, under the Presbyterian Church; Ottawa University, Franklin County, under the Baptist Church; Lincoln College, Topeka, belonging to the Congregational Church; a Female Seminary at Topeka under the Episcopal Church; and Wetmore Institute at Irving, under the Presbyterian Church. He adds that "the Methodists are erecting one at Circleville, in Jackson County, which will soon be ready for occupation; they also own Hartford Institute, at Hartford, Lyon County."

The history of Washburn College closely parallels that of the state. As early as 1858 plans were laid at a general meeting of the Congregational Association assembled at Manhattan for the founding of such an institution and Topeka was definitely chosen as the location in 1860. The Civil War interrupted such projects, and it was not until February 6, 1865, that the charter of the college, then known as Lincoln College, was granted.

When Harvey D. Rice, for whom the first building on the campus was named, went east to secure funds, Harriet Beecher Stowe gave him one thousand dollars. Three years after its incorporation, when Ichabod Washburn of Worcester, Massachusetts, presented the institution with a gift of $25,000, the name was permanently changed to Wasburn College. From its first location at Tenth and Jackson Streets, the college moved to the newly completed science hall in 1872. This building still houses some of the science laboratories.

In 1849 Dr. Charles Robinson went from Westport over the California trail to the Pacific slope. His road crossed the Wakarusa and wound over the low hill southeast of Mount Oread. Dr. Robinson climbed the hill on which the University of Kansas now stands and was deeply impressed by the outlook over the country. In 1854 when he returned to Kansas with Charles H. Brandscomb to select a site for the location of the emigrants sent out by the Emigrant Aid Company, they chose this same hilltop. Twenty-five tents were pitched on the north side of the hill and the emigrants ate their first meal near where the university buildings now stand. In a day or two they moved off the hill, camping near the Kaw River, and made plans for laying out the town. Robinson acquired Mount Oread and gave the site to the state for educational purposes.

The present home of the Kansas State College of Agriculture and Applied Sciences at Manhattan had its beginning in Bluemont College. It was chartered in 1858 and established a year later under the control of the Methodist Church. It laid claim to the right to become Kansas University when Kansas became a state, but the state government had determined to establish the present university at Lawrence.

Several members of the company that came to Kansas on the *Hartford* were college graduates. They agreed that a college should be established at Manhattan. The town donated one hundred lots toward the project and, through the sale of these and contributions received locally and in the east, sufficient money was raised to erect a building in 1859. The property was later deeded to the state and the present state school was opened in September, 1863.

FIRST LIBRARY
Vinland

CHASE COUNTY COURT-HOUSE
Cottonwood Falls

82

COAL CREEK LIBRARY, the first public library in Kansas, was started in the summer of 1859 when Anna Soule, a seventeen-year-old girl of Vinland, suggested to her friend, Martha Cutter, that they organize a literary society, patterned after one in New England. One object they had was to prevent dancing from becoming the only amusement of the community.

Twenty or thirty young people came to the meetings which were held every two weeks on the Cutter farm, at other houses and in log cabins. There was an hour of music, speaking pieces, and reading, followed by a social time.

At the first meeting someone proposed that they make it a library association. The members decided to have fifty-cent dues. As soon as they had accumulated ten dollars in their mite box, they sent to the Gift Association at Philadelphia for some books. Every book that came had a piece of jewelry attached to it. At the next meeting the jewelry was sold to make more money for the club. Anna bought a watch which, she claimed, never ran unless she did.

The members had other means of earning money for their library. One evening they put on an elaborate supper. Folks came from Prairie City and Palmyra (now Baldwin) and other nearby towns to attend. The profit to the club amounted to fifty dollars. This enabled them to greatly increase the size of the library and they again sent to Philadelphia for books.

Their selections were very good, including books by Harriet Beecher Stowe, the *Life of Charlotte Bronte*, various histories and a few popular novels.

From 1859 to 1875 the library was kept at the Cutter farm in Vinland and George Cutter was the first librarian. The books were then moved to the Grange hall, which served as the home of the library until 1900 when the association bought a lot and built a one-room structure for the purpose. This has been the library up to the present time. The building stands on the site of the old Cutter farm where the original library had its beginning. The present librarian, Miss Martha Cutter Kelley, is a great-niece of Anna Soule Prentiss who started it.

Anna's father had been induced by the Massachusetts Emigrant Aid Society to come out and help make Kansas a free state. He preempted a cabin on Coal Creek in 1854 and the rest of his family followed the next year when Anna was twelve.

She is credited with having decorated the first Christmas tree in Kansas. This was in 1862 when she was teaching in a primary school. There were no evergreen trees to be had, but her uncle, Professor Farnum, secured a forest tree and with Anna's assistance, trimmed its branches with the sprays from little arbor vitæ trees. The effect was quite realistic.

The first residents in that locality were George Cutter and William Barnes. The latter had been a nurseryman in Massachusetts. One year when Anna's brother was returning east for a visit, Mr. Barnes asked him to bring back to Kansas some cuttings of grapes. The boy brought in a carpet bag some amber grapes from Dracut, Massachusetts. Mr. Barnes was thus able to start quite a vineyard, the first one in Kansas. Because of this vineyard the place was called Vinland, the name it still retains.

Cawker City claims the distinction of having one of the first public libraries in the state. In 1874, soon after Cawker City was founded, a club of men was organized and took the name, "Hesperian Literary Club." The members paid five dollars each towards purchasing books which were kept in Smith and Tucker's law office. In 1883 a few women, desirous of enlarging the library and making it of interest to others, called a meeting. They offered to care for the two hundred volumes then upon the shelves and give voluntary attendance. Dr. Chapman gave the use of his building rent free for one year, and then offered to donate his valuable mineral collection providing the women would erect a building suitable for a public library and his museum.

The women were their own architects, transacting all the business themselves, and on July 4, 1885, they held ceremonial exercises dedicating the building. Miss Carrie Watson of the University of Kansas, who has compiled a history of Kansas libraries, says, "Cawker has more volumes in proportion to its population than any other place except libraries with state institutions."

Women in many other Kansas towns started libraries by gathering up a few old books from their neighbors; earning money for more by means of minstrel shows, chicken pie suppers, and fairs. They dusted and swept the rooms; distributed the books and catalogued them; and finally persuaded their fellow-townspeople to vote taxes and take the burden from their shoulders.

84

Through the efforts of women, libraries were established in Newton, Abilene, Republic, Ottawa, Eureka, Girard, Independence, Coffeyville, Iola, Leavenworth, McPherson, Yates Center, Baxter Springs, Pratt, Burlington and El Dorado.

The Atchison Public Library Association was organized, April 23, 1879. It was then and has ever since been composed entirely of women. One of the entertainments held to raise money was a fan drill given at Mrs. John J. Ingalls' home, which was then on the river bluff.

Eugene Ware presented the city of Fort Scott with a public library and as long as he lived there paid the expenses of maintaining it. The Topeka Free Library building was given by the Atchison, Topeka and Santa Fe and the Union Pacific Railroads.

In the fall of 1873 the library at Cottonwood Falls was about the livest concern in town, according to Carrie Breese Chandler. It had a capital of one thousand dollars and almost every family had shares, paid for in money or work. Books were selected with fine literary taste. The library was placed in the recorder's office in the new county court-house.

"To curl up in one of the deep windows of the roof story of the court-house," Mrs. Chandler says, "with *The Alhambra* or a sea tale by Captain Marryat was to be lost to the world. Sometimes you could look from the window across far east and see little dark figures running. They were antelope, but I never saw them nearer. Below those windows, on the cornice at the base of the mansard roof is a wide ledge. It seemed to be the favorite promenade of boys who went clear around the roof at an alarming pace. I have always thought it was a wonderful thing for children to grow up with such a beautiful example of architecture before their eyes. It was, and is yet, their measure of comparison."

The Chase County court-house was completed in 1873. It was built of limestone from a quarry west of the townsite and is in the Renaissance style of architecture of the period of Louis XIII. It has a basement, two stories and a cupola, extending 112 feet from the ground to the top of the flag-pole.

STATUE OF JOHN BROWN
Osawatomie

JOHN BROWN CABIN
Osawatomie

86

John Brown of Kansas

FIVE SONS of John Brown came to Kansas Territory from northern Ohio in 1854 and took up claims a few miles west of the present town of Osawatomie. They were known to be free-state advocates and were threatened by border ruffians. When John Brown heard of this he gathered up arms and ammunition and started for Kansas himself. After joining his sons here he became at once the leader of the free-state movement in that section. He insisted that the only way to stop the raids of the border ruffians was to conduct similar raids into the homes of the Missourians. His methods were violent ones. He twice returned to New England to get additional money and arms. On one of these trips a plan was evolved for establishing in the mountains of Virginia a stronghold which should serve as a refuge for escaped slaves.

Later financed by a group of anti-slavery leaders he settled on a farm near Harpers Ferry in what is now West Virginia. From this base he carried out his famous raid upon the United States Arsenal for the purpose of securing arms with which to outfit slaves for a general uprising. His men attacked the arsenal, October 16, 1859, captured it and held it for two days, finally succumbing to the superior strength of the United States Army. John Brown was taken, convicted of treason, and afterwards executed at Charleston.

The great stir he created did much to precipitate the Civil War. His zeal in a righteous cause led to violence which is not now perhaps considered justifiable, although one cannot fail to be impressed as someone has said, by "the tremendous earnestness of the man, by his extraordinary enterprise, by his courage and fortitude. He became a martyr whose name has been cherished in song and story as one who gave his life to make men free."

In the library, archives and museum of the Kansas State Historical Society is probably the largest collection of material relating to John Brown in existence. There are hundreds of his letters and papers, including one written by Brown to his father in 1849 in which he first expressed his views relative to slavery. His widow gave to the society a letter which Brown received from Victor Hugo as chairman of the French liberty committee, together with the gold medal presented to her as the widow of this champion of human liberty. There is a museum case filled with many intimate personal possessions, including a surveyor's compass and spy glass.

The John Brown Memorial State Park in the northwest part of

Osawatomie was dedicated, August 31, 1910, with Colonel Theodore Roosevelt as the speaker. It was here that the battle of Osawatomie was fought in 1856 when Brown led the townspeople against Missouri slaveholders. Twenty-one years later Senator John J. Ingalls spoke here in a ceremony commemorating those fallen in the battle.

A bronze statue of John Brown was unveiled in this park, May 9, 1935. Mounted on a pedestal of red, native Kansas stone, it represents the abolitionist bareheaded, in rough pioneer dress, with a musket strapped over his shoulder. The sculptor was George Fite Waters. It was erected through the efforts of the Women's Relief Corps of Kansas. Mrs. Anna L. January, who was in charge of the work, wrote a playlet that was given in various towns of the state to raise money for the statue.

Inscribed on the base are the following lines from Eugene F. Ware's poem on John Brown:

> *John Brown of Kansas:*
> *He dared begin,*
> *He lost,*
> *But losing won.*

In a little park on West Main Street is located Captain John Brown's Memorial Monument, a simple white shaft of Vermont marble, erected in 1877, and marking the burial ground of four men who gave their lives at the Battle of Osawatomie. The body of John Brown himself is buried at North Elba, New York.

The G. A. R. Post of Baldwin erected on the site of the battle of Black Jack near Baldwin a granite monument to commemorate the defeat of the border ruffian forces by the free-state men under John Brown. Here Captain Henry Clay Pate, a deputy United States marshal, with a band of Missourians had intended to capture Brown, but the ruffians were themselves taken prisoners.

The John Brown Cabin which stood originally about a mile and a half northwest of Osawatomie, has been moved to the State Park. This cabin belonged to Rev. S. L. Adair, brother-in-law of John Brown, but was Brown's home and headquarters during his stay in Kansas. It contains many historic relics and records pertaining to the colorful career of the abolitionist. In the main room is a cherry table on which Captain Brown wrote his letters.

The original cabin was built in 1854 by Samuel Glenn, a squatter, and bought soon after by Samuel L. Adair for two hundred dollars. It is of native logs taken from the banks of the Marais des Cygnes.

After the fighting and final retreat across the Marais des Cygnes by Captain Brown's men following the Battle of Osawatomie, the ruffians pillaged and burned all there was in the town at that time. The reason the John Brown cabin was not destroyed was because of the fact that Adair had taken into his home a man, woman, and three children, all of whom were sick with the fever. As they were too ill to leave their beds, the ruffians left saying they had not time to carry them out and they could not burn the cabin with them in it. The cabin is now housed in a modern building of stone, steel and glass, where its permanent protection is assured.

During Christmas day, 1858, eleven slaves taken out of Missouri by John Brown were concealed in the back room of the cabin. These slaves he escorted to Canada by way of the Underground Railway about a month later. After this daring exploit Brown did not again return to Kansas.

There were many stations which served as refuges for fleeing slaves as they awaited their next night's journey toward freedom. There was one at Lawrence, and another in Wakarusa. The last station south of Topeka was five miles southeast of Richland, at Twin Mound.

In Highland Park, east of Topeka, stands an old weather-beaten cabin which was used as a regular station for the Underground Railway. During the day the slaves hid in the cold, dark basement. Floors and walls were put together with hand-made, square wooden pegs. In the basement was the entrance to a tunnel used as a means of escape in case of emergency. This underground passage extended to the intersection of Fifteenth Street and the Shunganunga Creek.

Another station on the Underground Railway was near Holton in a vacant cabin on Spring Creek belonging to Dr. Albert Fuller. It was while John Brown was hiding here with slaves that a United States deputy marshal tried to capture him. A conflict ensued, called the Battle of the Spurs. The affair ended by Brown's party taking three prisoners, four horses, saddles, guns, pistols and other paraphernalia. Nine miles further on Brown stayed at the log cabin of Charles Smith on Gregg's Creek. The next station was sixteen miles farther, kept by John L. Graham. Soon the river was crossed at Nebraska City and they were in Iowa.

John Brown established in Anderson County a station on the Underground Railway near the base of Wadsworth Mound. This mound, commanding a view of several miles in all directions, offered a vantage point from which Brown frequently observed the operations of bands of proslavery men. About two miles north of the mound was another place of refuge for escaping slaves.

On the campus of Western University for Negroes at Quindaro is a statue of John Brown cut from Italian marble and mounted on a base of Vermont granite. This is the work of an Italian sculptor. The monument was unveiled in 1911. The entire cost of two thousand dollars was subscribed by negroes and the inscription reads: "Erected to John Brown by a Grateful People."

STATION ON UNDERGROUND RAILWAY
Highland Park

Prohibition in Kansas

THERE WAS BUT ONE LAW regulating liquor traffic in Kansas when it was admitted into the Union in 1861. This prohibited sales to Indians. The constitutional amendment providing state-wide prohibition became effective in 1881. For two or three years preceding the adoption, Kansas passed through a period of agitation. Temperance sentiment became a dominant force throughout the state. Prohibition became a political issue, a religious issue and a social issue. Many men and women were willing to go to almost any length to run saloon keepers out of the towns.

It was during this campaign that the women first came actively into the public affairs of Kansas. Women did not have the ballot here until 1912, and in 1880 their assumption of responsibility was somewhat resented. When the Women's Christian Temperance Union was organized in 1878 one of its objectives was to "do anything and everything right to secure the ballots of men, each one of which is more precious than gold."

The campaign for prohibition opened, August 21, 1879, with a twelve-day camp meeting in Bismarck Grove at Lawrence. Governor John P. St. John was there to deliver the address of welcome and to give his support to the campaign. He had become the titular leader of the dry element of the Republican party and was later considered the "father of national prohibition." The early home of John P. St. John is still standing in Olathe.

Carry A. Nation, ardent champion of prohibition, came from Texas to Medicine Lodge, Kansas, in 1890. Her first husband, Dr. Gloyd, had been a victim of alcoholism some years before, and this experience made her an implacable enemy of liquor. She saw the great advantage prohibition was to Kansas, even with all the treachery of officers who ignored the laws.

Through her efforts a chapter of the W. C. T. U. was organized in Medicine Lodge and she was appointed Jail Evangelist. Her duties were to visit the men in prison. She learned that almost everyone there was in jail directly or indirectly from the influence of intoxicating drinks. All said they got their liquor from Kiowa near the Oklahoma border.

Consequently it was in Kiowa that Mrs. Nation carried on her first saloon-smashing campaign, using stones and bricks. This aroused the

CARRY NATION'S HOME
Medicine Lodge

OLD BREWERY
Lawrence

people to such an extent that within two or three months all the dives in Barber County were closed.

The rum element in Medicine Lodge one night made an attack on Mrs. Nation's house, throwing rocks, breaking windows, and even threatening to burn the place. To this she replied, "Should my home be burned, it would be a lecture in favor of my cause that would be worth more to me than the home."

Mrs. Nation eventually sold her home at Medicine Lodge for eight hundred dollars and with the check made the first payment on a home for the wives of drunkards. She later added seven thousand five hundred dollars on its purchase and presented it to the Associated Charities in Kansas City, Kansas. It is now known as the W. C. T. U. Carry A. Nation Home.

An organization known as the Carry Nation Memorial Association has been chartered, the executive board of which includes old neighbors and children of neighbors of Carry Nation. They have arranged for the purchase of the former home of the dry crusader in Medicine Lodge and have marked it with a tablet. The house is to be restored as it was when Mrs. Nation started her hatchet crusade.

She cared nothing for display and had the most modest furnishings in her home. "I would feel like a reprobate," she said, "to fill my room with exquisite furniture, using money I could feed the hungry with, clothe the naked, doing things that would please my Lord. What a change! I used to delight in cut-glass, china, plush, velvet and lace. Now I can say 'vanity, all is vanity!' "

In Medicine Lodge Mrs. Nation is remembered as a church-going, outspoken woman. She devoted herself to helping the poor, often going from house to house to gather clothes for the destitute.

Many liquor men later confessed that their giving up of the liquor business and seeking honest work dated from Mrs. Nation's raids and their own conscious feeling of shame in their admiration of the courage of this lone woman.

It is said that a brewery in Lawrence was the first one closed when Kansas voted to become a dry state, and consequently was the first brewery to close in the United States. This brick building was erected in 1870 about a mile from the center of town by John Walruff, an early settler in Franklin County. He continued the manufacture and selling of beer for many years in violation of the prohibition law, but finally proceedings were begun against him and he was arrested and released on bail. He forfeited his bond and left the state, his family remaining in the large brick mansion which was worth some $10,000. The brewery stood empty and idle.

After many years as a fugitive from justice, Walruff returned to Lawrence, made some settlement with the county attorney, sold the brewery building and removed from the state. The new owner of the building used it for a thriving tannery business.

The old Weichselbaum brewery at Ogden on Highway 40 was built in 1871. It is situated at the foot of a hill which was tunneled out to allow storage space for beer. Heavily laden ox-carts carried the kegs away from the arched doorways in front of the building to points east and west. There is a well, covered by weathered planks. Here a horse was tied to a long wooden tongue and pumped water all day as he trod in a circle about the well.

An old brewery just east of Madonna Park in Council Grove was famous for its products in the '60s and '70s. It was used as a refuge for women and children during the Cheyenne Raid. A number of warriors entered the basement where there was a well, and demanded water instead of beer. It has since been converted into a residence.

W E ARE TOLD that of far more importance to the early settlers than the founding of towns was the establishment of mills. Samuel A. Johnson writes in the Kansas Historical Quarterly: "This was the activity upon which the Emigrant Aid Company concentrated its major efforts. The most urgent need of any isolated frontier community was a means of sawing lumber for building and of grinding grain for food. No better means could be found of encouraging the development of a community and of inflating the value of its real estate (from which the Aid Company hoped to derive a profit) than by locating in it a sawmill or grist mill."

The company is known to have located nine mills in Kansas — at Lawrence, Topeka, Manhattan, Osawatomie, Burlington, Wabaunsee, Atchison, Batcheller (Milford) and Claflin (Mapleton). All of these were operated by steam, and all but the one at Atchison were primarily sawmills. Grist mills were established in connection with those at Osawatomie, Manhattan, Wabaunsee and Milford.

On April 27, 1855, a group of eighty persons set out from Cincinnati with the intention of establishing a town in the Kansas Territory. They embarked on the *Hartford*, a sidewheel river steamer; went down the Ohio River to Cairo, up the Mississippi to St. Louis, thence along the Missouri to Kansas City, and up the Kansas River, finally unloading a short distance above the mouth of the Big Blue River. Here the town of Manhattan was established.

In planning for his return trip on the *Hartford*, the captain procured a cow and piled the deck high with wild hay. One day two Indians came aboard the craft and demanded tobacco. Not understanding the way of Indians, the captain ejected them from the boat with more speed than courtesy. The Indians then set fire to the grass along the banks and the fire soon spread to the hay on board the *Hartford*, which burned to the waterline. The bell and the boiler were saved. The bell hangs in the steeple of the Methodist Church in Manhattan and the boiler was purchased by the Emigrant Aid Company to run its Lawrence sawmill.

According to William E. Connelley, in "Kansas and Kansans," the first mill in the state was probably located at Auburn. This mill operated for the sawing of lumber during the day, and at night the burrs were turning to grind corn. The machinery was brought overland from Alton, Illinois, by John E. Moore and William Simmerwell.

OZAWKIE MILL

VALLEY FALLS MILL

96

The latter was a son of Robert Simmerwell, a missionary among the Pottawatomie Indians.

For about two years Frank M. Stahl, who later served as county treasurer and as chief of police in Topeka, was engineer at the mill. He was living with Robert Simmerwell. Young Stahl worked both day and night shifts, drawing double pay. White men and Indians came as far as one hundred miles to have their grain ground. Finally the mill was shut down.

The most picturesque mills in Kansas were the water mills, a few of which are still in use. There is one in Valley Falls built by a Polish immigrant, J. M. Piazzek, in 1855. The town was then known as Grasshopper Falls. While starting as a sawmill, the plant soon developed into a grist mill and later added a cotton gin. When the farmers began raising sheep a woolen mill was needed. Mr. Piazzek then built a two-story frame building and equipped it with machinery for making woolens and cotton.

These mills were run by water power from turbine wheels, all the mills being connected by cables. Many old belts made from buffalo skin are still in use. A three-story building started in 1878 was built of sandstone. When first taken from the earth the stone was soft enough to be sawed with a hand saw, and many of these sawed stones can be seen in the structure of the old mill.

The first electric light plant in Valley Falls was installed by Mr. Piazzek, who ran it by the same power that operated the mill. A son now owns the mill, enjoying a good custom grinding business.

In "Sunbonnet Days" Bliss Isely tells why the name of the town was changed from Grasshopper Falls to Valley Falls. It was in August, 1874, that the grasshoppers descended upon Kansas and stripped the fields of everything green.

"In a desperate effort to save the crops the Kansas legislature passed grasshopper laws." Mr. Isely says.* "One of them, which was as effective as any farm legislation I have ever known, had to do with the name of Grasshopper River which flowed across the prairie three miles southwest of our farm. It had once been a beaver stream and had been named Sautrelle River by the French trappers and traders who frequented it before the Louisiana Purchase. 'Sautrelle' being a French word meaning grasshopper, Lewis and Clark translated the name into English and so entered it on their charts in 1804. The legislature now

*Used by special permission of the copyright owners, The Caxton Printers, Ltd., 1935.

WATER MILL
Oxford

SODEN'S MILL
Emporia

98

changed the name of the Grasshopper to Delaware, and the town of
Grasshopper Falls became by a similar act Valley Falls. This ought to
have ended the grasshopper plague, only it did not."

The old red mill at Ozawkie was built in 1859 by Lewis Puder-
baugh. Here the government ground grain for the Delaware Indians
whose trail crossed the Delaware River at that point. Many arrowheads
have been unearthed on a knoll nearby and the redskins are known to
have used the oak grove west of the river for a camping ground.

It is fourteen years since the building has been used as a mill. Now
it merely provides storage space. One can see the massive oak beams
hewn with the adz and put together with wooden pins. The building
extended thirty feet farther west across the river until a few years ago,
when a portion was sawed off and fell into the water.

Soden's Mill in Emporia was built on the Cottonwood River in
1857 by three millwrights from Ohio. The land was owned originally
by Curtis Hyatt, who sold out the dam to Bill Soden, a wealthy
Scotchman, for one hundred dollars and returned to Ohio. The dam
was washed out by two floods in 1866, but was replaced. Today the
mill stands as a picturesque landmark on the banks of the river. There
are three sections, one of stone, the central part of brick and the other
of wood — all at different heights. The foundation is of stone. Across
the road is Soden's Grove where farmers formerly camped while their
grain was being ground.

An old mill dam building at Cottonwood Falls and the Alexander
Mill at Winfield are among those that have passed into oblivion. One
of the three mills of early days in Winfield still survives. It is a stone
building on the Walnut River, one of a chain of mills owned by the
Consolidated Flour Mills Company.

A drive over the rolling hills toward Paxico is well worth while, if
one winds up at Mill Creek just east of the village. There at the side
of the wide bridge in the cool shade of the woods stand the picturesque
ruins of an old water mill. The machinery is gone and the wheel no
longer turns in response to the movement of the water but the stone
building remains as a monument to the industry of the early pioneers.

The land on which the mill stands was purchased in 1879 from the
Pottawatomie Indians, whose wigwams could then be seen on every
side. The Indians themselves had a mill farther up the creek and it was
from this that Mill Creek received its name. The town itself was
named for one of the Pottawatomie braves.

During its prime the mill held an important place in the community, furnishing flour and feed to farmers and villagers within a radius of fifty miles. Mr. Strowig, who built it, operated it until about 1911 when conditions became unfavorable for smaller mills such as this and the one at Alma, both of which closed down at practically the same time.

Near Oxford is a mill built in 1874 of native limestone quarried from Sleigh's Hill about two miles north. It is run by water power, the water conducted through a sluiceway from a dam across the Arkansas River a mile or so away. This was one of the earliest mills in southeast Kansas. Oxford was settled about 1870.

The Oxford mill has had numerous owners since it was built. The original stones have been replaced by a modern roller process. Charles Champeny, the present owner, recalls the days when it was common for grist mills to operate without a cent's changing hands, a practice that has now been revived. For a sixty-pound bushel of wheat the farmer gets thirty-four pounds of flour. For a bushel of corn he gets thirty-five pounds of meal. The remainder is the mill's income. Some of the farmer customers live as far away as two hundred miles.

When in 1870 Bernard Warkentin came to Kansas and located at Halstead on the Little Arkansas River, he built a small water mill, but so little wheat was grown in that vicinity that he was at times forced to bring wheat from Atchison two hundred and sixty miles away to supply the tiny mill. Branching out from Halstead, he built the Newton mill and his expansion in the business was steady from that time on.

Much of the credit for making Kansas a great wheat state belongs to Mr. Warkentin, through whose efforts the first Russian hard winter wheat was introduced. He had a nominal association with the immigration department of the Atchison Railway and was largely influential in getting his countrymen, Mennonites from Russia, to settle in Kansas.

The Mennonites were well-to-do and there was not an illiterate person among them. They purchased farming land in 100,000-acre lots, taking most of it from the Santa Fe; this was railway grant land given the Santa Fe by the government as an inducement to build the railroad. The first party of Mennonites brought about thirty bushels of seed wheat from the Crimea. This seemed so well adapted to the soil and climate of Kansas that more was brought over and the acreage of the new wheat spread rapidly. Within less than twenty years the new variety had crowded out the older soft winter wheat and now it is the principal grain grown in Kansas.

In 1885 Mr. Warkentin began the importation of hard wheat for seed, direct from the Crimea, and since that time there have been various shipments from this variety's native habitat. At first millers in Kansas did not take kindly to the wheat; it was too hard for their burrs to crush. Later, methods were devised for steaming and making it soft enough to grind, but this was unsatisfactory, and it was not until the roller system of milling became general that the hard wheat took its place as the staple crop of central and western Kansas.

It is surprising to discover in Kansas a barn suggesting the attractive features of Gothic architecture in the form of buttresses. On the Brown dairy farm within view of the university buildings at Lawrence stands this picturesque structure beside an old stone mill, the farmyard surrounded by a crumbling rock wall.

Not until several years after the barn was built were the buttresses added to bolster up the sides which had begun to buckle. Passing motorists speculate as to their purpose and some have thought that a circus was once wintered here, the stone partitions making stalls for the animals.

Art students from the university often stroll out to the farm to sketch the old buildings. An artist from New York even honored the spot by depicting it on canvas, thus spreading abroad the fame of the buttressed barn.

Odell Shepard believes that throughout great stretches of America the barns are more important than the houses. "They are often larger, and usually they are more beautiful," he says in *The Christian Science Monitor*. "Their beauty is of that natural and honest kind that comes unsought and depends chiefly upon fitness to use . . . . Always and necessarily, the barn has been associated with labor, but it has been the center, also, of a quite surprising proportion of those merry-makings and junketings, now so nearly lost and forgotten, which have relieved the monotony of our rural life."

The quarry from which the stone was taken for the Kansas barn and the mill has been transformed into a pond where ducks and geese disport themselves and where cows can drink and wade on summer days.

Behind the barn is a taller building used originally for a grist mill. Constructed on the ledge of the stone quarry, it has a basement on the south, but is only two stories high on the north. It was built by William Brown in 1870. He had come to Kansas in 1859, survived the Quantrill raid in Lawrence and moved out to the farm eight years later.

101

He and his wife lived in the west part of the building, using the east side for the mill. The partitions have since been removed. The central floor served at one time for a dance hall, where all the young folk of the surrounding countryside made merry to the music of the violin and guitar.

Although there is still a mill here, it is run by electricity. In a large basement room the dairy supplies are kept. Two sons of the original owner, Elmer and Tom Brown, occupy frame cottages on the farm of sixty acres. In addition to the dairy farming they raise marketable fruit. For two years Elmer Brown served in the state legislature.

BUTTRESSED BARN
Near Lawrence

102

UCH OF THE CHARM of Holland is found in the rotating silhouettes of its windmills, filling the air with movement and sweeping the earth with the shadows of long-armed sails. Ever since the fifteenth century these busy wings have given to the Dutch landscape its singularly quaint character. In Kansas the picturesque form of the windmill creates even more of a sensation as a landmark because of its rarity.

The valley of the Platte River in Nebraska is said to be the backbone of the home-made windmill country of America. Farmers of South Dakota, Nebraska, Kansas and Oklahoma have found even the crudest of mills a luxury on the farm, lessening the burden of the work. This was especially true before modern mechanical devices came into general use. The windmill was used to pump water into tanks, to supply the house and barn, to drive cornshellers, feed mills, grindstones, woodsaws and even butter churns. In the pastures it supplied the grazing herds with water from deep-bored wells and furnished power to raise water for irrigating fields, gardens and orchards. The largest and most picturesque were, of course, those resembling the far-famed structures of "the land of flying gulls and flopping windmills."

The first mill builders were the worthy predecessors of the modern mechanical engineers. Their work called for inventiveness and constructive genius, and was the result of much experimenting and patient effort. Mills had a responsible task to perform and they played an important part in reclaiming the land and increasing the prosperity of the people. Their erect, sturdy bodies are like faithful watchers over the plains and they seem imbued with the indomitable spirit of their pioneer builders.

Early in the '60s a picturesque Swedish windmill loomed upon the horizon one mile west of Lawrence. Andrew Palm, a young man who had been a blacksmith in Sweden and was familiar with the construction of windmills in the old country, drew a picture of a windmill one day and showed it to his employer, John H. Wilder. Mr. Wilder became interested and the two formed a partnership. The editor of the first Lawrence newspaper was a co-worker in arousing interest in the scheme and obtained from a wealthy Englishman an investment of $10,000. Mr. Palm returned to Sweden and employed twelve men to come to America, build the mill, and work in it when it was completed.

Part of the mill was made in Sweden and brought to America. The mill-stones were brought from France and polished in New York.

LAWRENCE WINDMILL

The stone of the lower part was quarried at Lawrence, while the rest of the mill was built of wood that had been floated across from the north side of the river. The shingles, made by hand at a cost of ten dollars a thousand, were hauled from Chicago by ox-team.

All of the machinery was of wood except five or six little iron wheels, four of which were on the outside of the tower. Each fan was constructed of two great beams and many little pieces of wood. They embraced eighty feet in their swing.

The windmill was eighty feet high and contained five stories. The top story turned around so that the fans might catch the wind coming from any direction. Just above the basement was a balcony ten feet wide on which ran a windlass with a heavy chain around it, and attached to the movable top by a long braced beam.

Under the center of the building was a driveway running through the basement enabling the farmer to drive his load of grain in out of the weather. In answer to a message shouted to the miller above through a speaking tube, an elevator could be let down directly into the wagon. Thus, without dumping or shoveling, the load was transferred to the stones above or to the storage bins on either side.

There were two burrstones, one for corn and one for wheat. Each could grind twenty bushels a day, an unprecedented feat in the west where the mill was considered a wonder. For a few years it furnished power for a wagon and plow shop, and was in constant use until 1885. Its largest business was during the Civil War. Farmers came from hundreds of miles away, camping in wagons while awaiting their turn.

Mr. Palm and Mr. Wilder formed a partnership, calling the firm "The Windmill Agricultural Company." They employed twenty-five or thirty men.

High upon the bluffs overlooking Lawrence this windmill was a most distinctive landmark and plans were being made for its permanent preservation when it was unfortunately destroyed by fire in 1905. Only a few crumbling ruins of the crude masonry of the stone foundation remain to mark the spot.

Other picturesque windmills have dotted the state. One was in Pfeifer, a little Russian community near Hays. This mill was torn down five years ago, leaving only the foundation and the heavy burrs lying on the ground in an empty field.

A comparatively modern Dutch type of windmill, dating back to 1882, stands at Reamsville, fifteen miles northwest of Smith Center. This was erected by Charles G. Schwarz, formerly of Michelenberg,

WAMEGO WINDMILL

REAMSVILLE WINDMILL

106

Germany, who landed in Philadelphia during the centennial, and came to Smith County to take up a homestead. With his old-country training in the milling industry, he conceived the idea of constructing a mill to be run by harnessing the wind for his motive power. He first cut a pair of burrs out of native stone, sharpening them by hand with a small iron pick. One of these burrs forms the stepstone at the west door of the now abandoned mill.

Mr. Schwarz and a brother sawed the heavy logs for the upright posts with what was called a ship-saw. Conrad H. A. Schwarz, a son of the builder, describes the process as follows: "One stands on top of the log or square-hewn timber and one underneath with a chalk line to mark the saw cut. The saw is pulled up and down to cut the plank. All of the heavy planks and heavy sawn timbers, also 4 by 4's, 6 by 8's, etc., came by way of this sawmill. There was no machine in the country for cutting timber, and, had there been, there was no money to pay for such work."

The mill is octagonal in shape, forty feet in diameter at the bottom, tapering to eighteen feet at the top. On the fifth floor was a large wheel with wooden cogs, also home-made. A tail-wheel, ten feet in diameter, was built in such a way as to turn the planes of the big wheel to the wind. The first fans were blown off by a severe blizzard and wind-storm that struck suddenly, January 12, 1887. The main shaft to which the fans were fastened was a white elm log squared to twenty-four inches. It broke where it was rounded for the bearing and the four fans all came down. During the following summer Mr. Schwarz rebuilt the shaft and fans from pine timbers hauled up from Gaylord, twenty-five miles away.

Corn and graham flour were ground on shares and the corn meal was said to be of such excellent quality that it was sold in all adjacent towns in Kansas and Nebraska. At the foot of the mill Mr. Schwarz built a "soddy" where he lived for many years. The mill has not been running for a long time, but its huge bulk still dominates the landscape for miles around and attracts many visitors.

Built after the manner of the mills of Holland was that at Wamego, which has been preserved by appreciative citizens in the little park adjoining Highway U. S. 40. This heritage dates back to 1879. It was built by a Hollander, J. B. Schonhoff, from red sandstone on his farm. A crude home-made forge served for hammering out all of the machinery but the main shaft; and for harnessing the Kansas winds, a huge fan, forty feet in diameter, was constructed, almost sweeping the ground in its revolutions. This mill brought to its owner during twenty years a profitable income through a custom grinding business. Then for years it stood idle, serving as a storage and ice house, and even a chicken-house. Some time ago, A. M. Bittman and T. J. Leach, members of the park board, supervised the moving of the structure twelve miles to its present location in Wamego.

Each stone was marked and the place it occupied designated, in order that each might be replaced in its original position. A special day, known as "Park Day," was set aside for moving the mill. Thirty-five teams and trucks were lent by farmers of the surrounding country and women served lunch in the park for the men workers. That was in 1924. A mound was built for a foundation through the voluntary aid of an engineer of the Union Pacific Railway Company. A relief portrait of Ceres, the goddess of grain, occupies a conspicuous place above the door. Park officials intend to put the gear in shape, set the old burrs in their places and equip the mill with great vanes so that they may turn as they did before. It will then again be a replica of hundreds that rotate along the Zuyder Zee where Schonhoff learned the technique of grinding grain.

America's oldest windmill of quaint Dutch architecture was moved several times in a similar way and is now installed in the Henry Ford museum of early Americana at Dearborn, Michigan. Built at Sandwich, on Cape Cod, just thirteen years after the Pilgrims landed, it was moved to South Yarmouth, Massachusetts, in 1750, and again to Bass River in 1782. There it remained, doing its share of the Cape's grinding until 1894, when it was taken to West Yarmouth. Souvenir-hunters were said to have offered as high as five dollars for a shingle at the time it was dismantled for shipment to Detroit. Every shingle and stone was carefully taken down, checked, and "filed" away under police guard to be used in rebuilding the mill in its original shape.

Early Bridges

A BRIDGE is as much a landmark as is a church or an old mill. Distances are measured from it. The native of the neighborhood will direct the inquiring stranger to "the third house beyond the bridge," or the "last building before you come to the bridge."

There is a certain fascination about any bridge, whether wooden, stone, or iron, and few people in passing over one can resist the impulse to pause for a moment to lean on the parapet and look down into the water. Of course one does find such unappreciative individuals as the tourist who stood on an old stone bridge, gazing thoughtfully into the dry bed twenty feet below.

"Now why doesn't this community take some action on this thing?" he said. "If we had it in my town we'd either buy a river or sell the bridge."

Spanning the Wakarusa River near Berryton is a triple-arched stone bridge built in 1878 on the township line between Williamstown and Monmouth Townships. It is on the state road leading from Topeka to Quenemo. George Washington Berry, for whose son Berryton was named, was influential in establishing the state road and in securing the public appropriation for building the bridge. It was one of the first bridges of this permanent type of architecture to be erected in Kansas.

Wakarusa Creek or River received its name before the day of bridges, according to an Indian legend which says that a maiden sought to cross the stream on horseback. As she proceeded, the waters became deeper and deeper until her body was half immersed, when she exclaimed, "Wakarusa!" meaning hip deep. She passed over in safety.

There was a famous crossing of the Santa Fe Trail over the Neosho River at Council Grove. The first bridge was of heavy oak timber sawed out of trees in the original Council Grove about 1860. Used for a time as a toll bridge, it is remembered as the only bridge that far west in the state.

Old bridge piers at De Soto, Kansas, tell of the time when it was thought that De Soto would be a station of the Kansas Pacific Railroad. But with the building of the stone piers the work on the bridge ended, partly for lack of funds, and partly because the builders saw the futility of the project.

Covered bridges in Kansas are very rare. The two that remain today in Leavenworth County retain some of that rough and hardy character that belonged to the first settlers of Kansas. These patched

JARBALO BRIDGE
Leavenworth County

SPRINGDALE BRIDGE
Leavenworth County

110

and weather-beaten relics of the days of the horse and buggy are found spanning Stranger Creek. One is at Springdale and the other at Jarbalo, both remote from the much-traveled highways, but capable of performing for many years to come the services for which they were designed.

The timbers of the bridge at Springdale were hand-hewn from trees nearby and laid upon stone abutments. A more or less intricate pattern of wooden arches and criss-cross trusswork supported the sides, which were painted red. The shingled roof was designed to protect the huge beams from the ravages of the weather. On rainy days this dark shelter made an ideal place to play, as well as a haven for travelers caught in a sudden shower. The floor planks rattled under wheels and hoofs and in summer the thick, cool dust was soft on a boy's bare feet.

Those who are acquainted with covered bridges recall the warm shelter in winter and the cool shade in summer while water lapped refreshingly underneath. One of the chief thrills of crossing a covered bridge, it is said, was "the quick run through, with carefully held breath and a wish just as carefully held in thought."

Among the unique radio sound effects produced in the studios nowadays is that of a four-horse coach rocking its way through a covered bridge. Six men are required to gain the proper effect, two crushing peanuts, one jingling sleigh bells, one operating a racket device, one drumming with his fingertips on a sounding board, and one rolling a wooden keg around.

The John Bell Bridge, as that near Jarbalo is called, is more than one hundred and fifty feet long. On the pine rafters hundreds of mud-dauber wasps have built their nests. This bridge, built in 1866, was an important link in the once well-traveled "Leavenworth to Perryville" road. Before its completion travelers had been forced to ford Stranger Creek several miles downstream, an impossibility during times of high water.

Stranger Creek is mentioned by many early explorers and travelers. It was called O-keet-sha by the Kansas Indians, meaning "stranger" or "wandering aimlessly about." Along its banks lone fishermen often sat patiently in flat-bottomed boats angling for catfish.

Until last fall when it was torn down, another covered bridge spanned this creek. It was at Easton, a few feet north of the ford or crossing that was part of the Oregon Trail. The wagon trains outfitted for the northwest at Fort Leavenworth, and Stranger Creek was the first stop. This bridge was built in 1856 by engineers under the direc-

ARCHED BRIDGE
Shawnee County

BRIDGE OVER WAKARUSA RIVER
Near Berryton

112

tion of Colonel Albert Sydney Johnston, who was then in command at Fort Leavenworth. He later became one of the most noted leaders of the Confederate Army in the Civil War. Many great expeditions, military and otherwise, passed over this bridge.

The town of Easton was founded in 1855 by Armistead Dawson, who had previously operated a trading post and ranch on the military road at that point. The town was once a rendezvous of the proslavery border ruffians and many exciting incidents occurred there. Near the bridge Mr. B. Frank Flory who lived in the vicinity in early days picked up an Indian tomahawk which was the nucleus of what afterward became a fine collection of Indian relics which he now has at his home in York, Pennsylvania. A fourth covered bridge near Farmington, above Easton, was torn down several years ago.

There is considerable romance associated with the spanning of the Kansas River. Many interesting details are given in a historical sketch by F. W. Giles, an early settler.

The town of Tecumseh had in 1855 secured the first charter for a company to bridge the Kansas River under the title of "Kaw River Bridge Company," and had exclusive rights for bridging the stream at any point within five miles of that village. When the existence of this charter came to be known at Topeka, some apprehensions were aroused that its purpose was not only to facilitate the erection of a bridge at Tecumseh, but also to prevent the erection of one at Topeka, under the plea that the ground was covered by the five-mile limitation; and there can be no doubt that such was the intention of the legislature in its zeal to promote the prosperity of proslavery Tecumseh as against free-state Topeka.

On the fourteenth of February, 1857, a charter was obtained for a bridge to be built at Topeka, with a capital of one hundred thousand dollars. Its rights were limited to the "building and maintaining of a bridge across the Kansas River at any point upon said river no less than five miles nor more than ten miles above the village of Tecumseh." A bridge was felt to be the most valuable acquisition in advancing the growth of the town of anything that could be reasonably hoped for, and the possibility of obtaining one was a frequent theme of discussion among the corporators and citizens during the summer of 1857.

One evening a meeting of the trustees and stockholders of the Topeka Bridge Company was held, and a proposal was made by a new company to erect a passable bridge for $10,000 — the distance from shore to shore being nearly one thousand feet.

113

The plan was to drive oak piling in sections, these to be strengthened by diagonal braces nailed upon each side, the braces being of cottonwood planks, two inches thick and six inches wide. Upon the sections was to be placed a twelve by twelve oak cap into the head of each pile; then cottonwood stringers from pier to pier upon them. This plan was well suited to the conditions. The contract was concluded, and on the first day of May, 1858, two months in advance of the stipulated date, the bridge was completed from shore to shore, 925 feet in length—the first that ever spanned the Kansas River.

Citizens of Topeka were exultant over the accomplishment of the enterprise. As an indication of their feeling, the following extract from an editorial in the Kansas Tribune of May 8, 1858, is given:

"The completion of the bridge across the Kaw River at this place has opened one of the greatest thorofares of the west. The tide of travel across the river at this point is increasing daily and hourly, and at the present rate will soon become a volume of moving humanity, unprecedented in all previous migratory movements.

"Besides the local travel for miles up and down the river, which is itself very considerable, this is the point of crossing for all the trains for Southern and Southwestern Kansas, New Mexico, Arizona, California, and much of the travel to Utah and Oregon. Several trains have already crossed going to and coming from Santa Fe, and also going to California. Many of them have herds of cattle, which it is very troublesome and expensive, as well as dangerous, to ferry over such a stream as the Kaw with its swift current and shifting bed. The bridge is 900 feet long, 16 feet wide, and twenty emigrant teams of 250 head of cattle can pass upon it at the same time with safety and convenience, so that not a moment of time is necessarily lost.

"With such a convenience as this for crossing, emigrants to all parts of the south and west will not be long in finding their way hither, judging, and correctly too, that a few miles of extra travel to such a perfectly safe and speedy crossing is cheaper than the risk to their teams and goods on a frail boat liable at any moment to the hidden dangers of this capricious stream."

This bridge was in the same locality as those that have succeeded it. In the month of July, rains of unusual frequency and magnitude occurred throughout the region drained by the Kansas River, and a rise in that stream followed. By the middle of the month the water had attained a height and was bearing down a mass of flood water that caused deep apprehension for the safety of the bridge.

114

All day on the 16th, numbers of men were upon the bridge, working in every possible way to relieve it from the vast pressure of trees, stumps, roots, and the general mass of drift that had caught upon the piers. And still the waters rose, so that by nightfall they were within three feet of the flooring of the bridge. All through the night, with a flood of rain pouring upon them, men with ropes, picks, axes, and levers labored to save this greatest hope and pride of the little town. At about nine o'clock the next morning, the water and drift reached the flooring of the bridge; it was lifted from the piers, and in sections swung down the stream.

Two of the men kept their positions upon the heaving, cracking wreck and started to float away with it. They skipped from timber to plank, till the fragments floated sufficiently near the shore to allow them to swim to terra firma.

After July, 1858, the primitive mode of crossing streams by ferry was again resorted to at Topeka, and little was said about bridging the Kaw for the succeeding period of seven years. Finally a company was incorporated to build a pontoon bridge, and it was completed in 1865, less than three months before the neigh of the first iron horse from Kansas City west was heard in this part of the valley.

Over this bridge all of the stone and most of the building materials used in the construction of the east wing of the State-house were transported from the depot by mules and horses in the latter '60s. The pontoon was successfuly used for several years, but was washed out by a flood on July 4, 1869. An iron bridge succeeded this one — a toll bridge, which lasted until the present steel-cement structure was erected.

George A. Root, curator of archives for the Kansas Historical Society, has found the official records of four hundred ferries known to have operated under license in Kansas, carrying traffic across the streams and rivers before the day of bridges. There were 103 licenses issued for the Kansas River alone. The first ferry established in Kansas was the Mose Ginter ferry about eight miles west of the mouth of the Kaw. It was functioning as early as 1831. Not since 1885 have ferries been operating in Kansas except at scattered points along the Missouri River and during flood emergencies when bridges were washed away.

OLDEST TREE IN TOPEKA
Huntoon and Clay Streets

COTTONWOOD TREE
On Capitol Grounds

116

*T*HE TREE is at once a contemporary object and an antique. Red cedars still standing in Pottawatomie County were sheltering papooses when the Pilgrim Fathers landed on Plymouth Rock. The first settlers in Kansas found timber along the river valleys, and the whine of the sawmill was the first industrial voice heard in the eastern half of the state.

Wagons and buggies of early days were repaired with hickory, ash and pecan. The bur-oak furnished wood for fence posts. Enormous sycamores along the bottom lands provided frames and other parts of a house or barn not in contact with the weather. The hackberry, elm and cottonwood have served for the construction of many buildings of historic note throughout the state.

On the western plains during the '80s it was possible for home-steaders to preempt an additional quarter section of land by the simple expedient of planting forty acres of trees on it. This second tract was known as a "tree claim." It was often planted with black locusts which were known to stand the semi-arid climate characterizing the region. Little clumps of slender trees resulting from these timber tracts can be seen today standing alone on the prairie.

Kansans owe much to the cottonwood that made quick growth despite the dry soil of the plains. The first towns set out rows of them along their main streets, irrigating with water hauled in barrels from nearby streams. Leading into Garden City are two roads lined on either side with large cottonwoods, their interlaced branches forming beautiful canopies.

A huge cottonwood west of Englewood, thirty-one feet in circumference, was already of great size when the first white settlers located there. At Oswego another cottonwood stood in the center of one of the important streets, serving as a favorite resting place until February, 1936, when it was cut down. It had become so old and decayed that it was considered unsafe. Part of the trunk has been made into a desk for the mayor.

On the southeast corner of the State-house grounds in Topeka stands a giant cottonwood, one of the largest and most beautiful trees in Kansas. It is approximately ninety feet high and has a spread of nearly two hundred feet. There are several stories as to its origin. One is to the effect that it grew out of one of the stakes, brought up from the Kansas River during the construction of the capitol, to be used

117

for guy ropes to anchor the derricks in elevating the massive stones. When workmen cleared away the debris it is said the stake was found growing and so was protected and saved.

Others say that the tree grew from a seed that had blown onto the grounds. A former janitor and custodian of the State-house lawn recalls having brought a cottonwood sapling up from the Shunganunga Creek and transplanted it to the capitol grounds the year before work was begun on the State-house. Later he wired boards around the tree to protect it from workmen and teams. This tree he believes to be the famous old cottonwood now standing.

On Topeka's first Arbor Day, April 23, 1875, more than seven hundred trees were planted on the capitol square. A parade with men carrying trees on their shoulders preceded the actual tree setting. The fire department turned out in full force to furnish water. Trees were planted so thickly that in later years they had to be thinned out. During Governor Morrill's administration an appropriation was secured to beautify the State-house lawn and a landscape gardener was brought from New England. He would have cut down the cottonwood tree had it not been for the urgent insistence of a group of men who had grown to love it.

Former presidents Harrison, McKinley and Taft made campaign speeches beneath this tree and under it the Twentieth Kansas Regiment of volunteers assembled. After making a record in the Philippines, the regiment and its commander bade farewell under its branches. The tree is said to have been a great favorite with the late senators, John J. Ingalls and Preston B. Plumb. It is as dear to hearts of the Jayhawkers as is the Washington Elm to the people of Cambridge.

The late Charles Curtis was here notified of his nomination for the Vice-presidency and under its branches great crowds gathered, July 23, 1936, to witness the notification of Governor Alfred M. Landon of his nomination for the Presidency of the United States.

Some miles west of Topeka stands a cottonwood tree, the silhouette of which bears a marked resemblance to a Dutch windmill. As it grows year after year it preserves this unusual form, fashioned originally by the wind itself.

An old locust tree that figured in Margaret Hill McCarter's *The Price of the Prairie* is located in Topeka. In early days it was the only tree within a radius of three miles from Shunganunga Creek to the Kansas River. Pupils of the third grade of Central Park School placed under it in 1912 a cement block inscribed with these words: "The oldest tree in Topeka."

On West Loula Street in Olathe once grew a maple tree under which the Delaware and Wyandotte Indians are said to have made a treaty of peace. In 1905 the city council and street department decided this tree would have to come down since it stood in the way of a proposed sidewalk. Mrs. Jennie Baker and her daughter, on whose property the tree stood, marched round and round it to prevent the men with axes from doing their work of destruction. Three-fourths of the population of Olathe came to their assistance and protected the tree until legal aid was obtained for its preservation.

Another "treaty tree" that has been spared the ax and come to a ripe old age is the Council Oak in Council Grove under which a treaty of peace was signed between the United States and the Osage Indians, August 10, 1825, giving the white men unmolested use of the Santa Fe Trail across the great plains. The town received its name at this council. This tree, said to be three hundred years old, is one of the relics of an old oak grove which covered a large part of the bottom land east of the Neosho River. George C. Sibley, one of the three United States commissioners who signed the treaty, in describing the affair years afterward, said that he gave the town its name and had "Big John" Walker, one of his men, carve the name of Council Grove on a large oak standing near their tent.

A little farther west stands the Post Office Oak where trailers left messages for incoming and outgoing wagon trains. At the base was a cache for that purpose. The tree was located on the old camp ground of the trailsmen, now known as Madonna Park.

General Custer camped under an elm tree at Council Grove in 1867. When an enterprising street commissioner arranged with a wood-chopper to remove this tree for the wood it would furnish, it was saved by Mrs. W. A. McCollum, who gave the man ten dollars in lieu of taking the life of this historic sentinel of the forest. She then went to the city council and secured its consent to save the tree forever by a protecting resolution which the council passed.

Among the four famous old Kansas trees that have been added to the American Forestry Association's hall of fame for trees are the Council Oak, the Post Office Oak and the Custer Elm. The other is the Lincoln Memorial tree at Atchison, marking a spot where Abraham Lincoln once spoke. This tree is no longer standing, however.

A Washington Friendship Grove has been established in

POST OFFICE OAK
Council Grove

CUSTER ELM
Council Grove

120

Madonna Park in Council Grove from horse-chestnuts taken from the famous Friendship Tree near Bath, Pennsylvania. This tree, which has a circumference of twenty-seven feet at the base of the trunk, was presented by George Washington to his friend, General Robert Brown, of the Continental Army in 1785. Washington is said to have dug the seedling from his garden in Mount Vernon. The horse-chestnut trees at Mount Vernon were presented to Washington by General "Light Horse Harry" Lee, illustrious soldier of the Revolutionary Army. Other "Washington Friendship Groves" have been established in various states and possessions of the United States.

On May 10, 1930, a Kansas Mothers' Tree planting ceremony was held in Council Grove, sponsored by the Council Oak chapter of the D. A. R. This tree was awarded to Council Grove by Miss Barbara Bayne, tree historian of America. It is a white birch. Soil from the base of the four previously planted Mothers' Trees, in Pennsylvania, Washington, D. C., California and Texas, was placed at its roots as it was planted by the side of the statue, The Madonna of the Trail. This statue is one of twelve erected by the D. A. R., marking the route of the National Old Trail across the continent. It represents a pioneer mother with a babe in her arms and a small child clinging to her skirts.

The Kit Carson Tree, an elm near Halstead on the bank of Black Kettle Creek, served as a marker for travel for the Arapahoe and Osage Indian hunters. According to a local story, it was here that Kit Carson and his band of emigrants camped for a night. At three o'clock in the morning the yells of the Comanche Indians were heard in the surprised little camp. Kit Carson led in the defense against the Indians, of whom Chief Black Kettle and Chief Hard Hope were the commanders. The ammunition of the white men was running low and the Indians were formed for a final charge when a company of United States cavalry, commanded by General Custer, dashed to their relief and the Indians were forced to retreat.

More than eighty years have passed since the Old Signal Oak, a historic tree north of Baldwin, served as a beacon tower from which a lantern was swung to call together the members of the free-state band who lived in that vicinity. It was located on Big Hill. During the '50s two bands of free-state men at Blue Mound and Big Hill joined themselves together in the free-state cause. Lantern signals were used when the men were in need of reenforcements. A portion of the oak has been fashioned into two gavels, one of which was used by the national chairman of the Republican convention at Kansas City in 1928.

COUNCIL OAK
Council Grove

A large elm tree on the east bank of the Neosho River, southeast of Chanute, was used years ago as the starting point in the survey for a township road. Marked by three notches on the north side, it still stands to guide surveyors in remarking the route. Such a sentinel was often called a "bound" tree because it marked a boundary of land or property. It was apt to be mentioned in the deed to the land.

The first newspaper in Kansas was printed under the shade of a towering elm in Leavenworth, September 15, 1854. The editor, William H. Adams, was the spokesman for a few squatters who had crossed the Missouri River on a ferry and sought to make Kansas pro-slavery. His paper was called the Kansas Herald.

It was under an oak tree at Morehead on the Missouri River near Highland that the first Masonic lodge in Kansas was organized. This lodge is still known as Smithton, No. 1, named in honor of John W. Smith. Wood from the tree has been made into gavels.

The Lone Tree on the banks of Crooked Creek in Meade County marks the site of the last assault of the Indians upon surveying parties in Kansas. In 1874 six men in the Short surveying party were massacred by a band of Cheyennes near the tree under which the surveyors had pitched their camp.

Many years ago thirty Vermonters settled in Kansas on the Little Osage River in Bourbon County where all took claims. A quarter section of land was selected for a town site and, because of the large number of maple trees in that place, the name Mapleton was chosen. There is an old tavern at Mapleton, three stories in height, built entirely of black walnut — frame, siding, shingles and interior finish — all grown along the Osage River. There are rail fences of black walnut. The wood is said to be so pure chemically that it is free from decay.

Wakeeney is called the "honey locust town." In the courthouse park alone there are at least two hundred locusts and nearly all of the street trees are of the same kind.

During the year of the Washington Bicentennial there was a nation-wide movement to plant trees as a fitting memorial to our first President. Kansas had her part in the celebration and several communities had tree-planting ceremonies. The Emporia chapters of the D. A. R. and the Daughters of American Colonists presented eight elm trees to the city. These were planted in Hammond Park. The Woman's Kansas Day club gave an Austrian pine which was planted on the State-house grounds in Topeka. A horse-chestnut was also planted there by the Colonial Dames of America in Kansas.

FIRST OIL WELL
Neodesha

THE FIRST OIL WELL west of the Mississippi and east of California to yield oil in commercial quantity was the Norman No. 1 discovery well near the east edge of Neodesha on the bank of the Verdigris River. It was drilled by William M. Mills, a pioneer of the western fields.

Mr. Mills, a native of Pennsylvania, grew up in the oil fields of that state in the days when the "oil country" meant Pennsylvania, New York, Ohio and West Virginia. After prospering in eastern oil fields for a while, he emerged penniless from the Bradford, Pennsylvania, oil exchange. Then, with his wife, he started out in a horse-drawn buggy for the west, where a few adventurous spirits were beginning to suspect that petroleum riches lay below the fertile Kansas soil.

The record of his adventures is given as follows in the *Stanolind Record*. He finally inspired enough confidence in his activities to receive financial encouragement, particularly from a doctor, a banker, and two druggists who wished to procure a source of natural gas for Neodesha.

Desiring to drill his test well in or near the town, he accepted the offer of T. J. Norman, a blacksmith of Neodesha, to use his four-acre tract just outside the eastern boundary. Here in Mr. Norman's garden patch Mr. Mills drilled in search of gas in 1892, an act which was destined to mark the beginning of a new oil empire. The well was shot and completed, October 4, 1893. The initial production was twelve barrels a day.

About a mile from the No. 1 Norman Mr. Mills drilled his second well, the No. 1 J. K. Demoss, and got another producer. With a two-ounce bottle of Kansas oil as convincing evidence of Kansas' productivity, he sought financial help in the East and succeeded in interesting John H. Galey of Pittsburgh.

In 1894 Mr. Mills sold his interest in the venture to Guffey and Galey for $4,000 and returned to the home he had established in Osawatomie, where he devoted the rest of his life to natural gas interests.

The No. 1 Norman was abandoned in 1933 and the casing pulled. This casing was on exhibition at the Tulsa Oil Exposition in 1936. Nothing remains at the site of the old well but two posts. Plans are being made to place a marker on the location of this famous test well and to erect a monument in the center of town where passing motorists may view a reminder of Kansas' pioneer oil days.

125